Microcomputer Resource Book
for
Special Education

Microcomputer Resource Book for Special Education

Dolores Hagen

Reviewed and commended to the field by
The Council for Exceptional Children

A Reston Computer Group Book

Reston Publishing Company, Inc.
A Prentice-Hall Company
Reston, Virginia

Library of Congress Cataloging in Publication Data
Hagen, Dolores.
   Microcomputer resource book for special education.

   1. Handicapped children—Education—Data processing.
2. Computer-assisted instruction. 3. Microcomputers.
I. Title.
LC4019.H33   1984   371.9′028′54   83-17651
ISBN 0-8359-4345-3
ISBN 0-8359-4344-5 (pbk.)

Copyright 1984 by
Dolores Hagen

All rights reserved. No part of this book may be
reproduced in any way, or by any means, without
permission in writing from the author.

10   9   8   7   6   5   4   3   2   1

Printed in the United States of America

To Marc
and all children who need technology for a better life

Trademarks Used in Microcomputer Resource Book for Special Education

Apple is a registered trademark of Apple Computer, Inc.
Apple II is a registered trademark of Apple Computer, Inc.
Apple IIe is a registered trademark of Apple Computer, Inc.
Apple II Plus is a registered trademark of Apple Computer, Inc.
Apple III is a registered trademark of Apple Computer, Inc.
Apple Cat II is a registered trademark of Novation, Inc.
Atari is a registered trademark of Atari, Inc.
CBM is a registered trademark of Commodore Business Machines
CCD is a registered trademark of Hartley Courseware, Inc.
Commodore is a registered trademark of Commodore Business Machines
CP/M is a registered trademark of Digital Research Corp.
DEC is a registered trademark of Digital Equipment Corp.
Diablo is a registered trademark of Xerox Corp.
Echo II is a registered trademark of Street Electronics
H-89 is a registered trademark of Zenith Radio Corp.
Hartley Courseware is a registered trademark of Hartley Courseware, Inc.
Heath is a registered trademark of Zenith Radio Corp.
IBM is a registered trademark of International Business Machines
PET is a registered trademark of Commodore Business Machines
TI99/4A is a registered trademark of Texas Instruments
Timex/Sinclair 1000 is a registered trademark of Sinclair Research, Ltd.
TRS-80 Model I, II, III are registered trademarks of Tandy Corp.
VIC-20 is a registered trademark of Commodore Business Machines
VisiCalc is a registered trademark of VisiCorp
Vox Box is a registered trademark of Tandy Corp.
Zenith is a registered trademark of Zenith Radio Corp.
64 is a registered trademark of Commodore Business Machines
800 is a registered trademark of Atari, Inc.

Contents

	Introduction ix
I	**Overview** 1
	General Rules To Finding Software 5
	Communications 8
	Environmental Control 10
	Future 12
II	**Hints For Implementation** 14
	Motivation 18
	Individual Needs Met by Software 21
	Self Expression 27
III	**Specific Disabilities** 31
	Learning Disabled 33
	Deaf and Hearing Impaired 41
	Blind and Visually Impaired 49
	Mentally Retarded 53
	Physically Handicapped 58
IV	**Logo** 65
V	**Communication** 72
	On-Line Services 73
	Instructional Services 76
	Educational/Career Enhancement 80

Contents

VI   The Common Denominators   83

VII   Future   89
- The Real Future   94
- A Personal Reflection   96

Appendices   98

- A. Software Publishers and Distributors   99
- B. Selected Software for Special Education   138
- C. Physically Handicapped   158
- D. Blind   168
- E. Authoring Systems   172
- F. Administration   179
- G. Special Hardware Selections   184
- H. On-Line Services   189
- I. Logo   191
- J. Print Resource   199

Index   203

Introduction

Microcomputers are tools. They are a means to an end, just like any other tool devised by man. How effective the tool is, in the hands of the user, depends on the training and understanding that person has of the tool.

Today, a vast majority of the formal training to use a microcomputer is identified as some form of "computer literacy." One of the problems with this term is trying to find two people who agree on its meaning. In the view of some, it means an understanding of, and programming in, several computer languages. To others it means BASIC programming with a large portion of "computer history" thrown in. In very rare instances it can mean being a computer user.

It makes for interesting conjecture to think what rush-hour traffic in Los Angeles would be like if all the instruction for drivers' training classes had been "History of the American Auto Industry" or "How to Build a Carburetor" instead of user skills. Unfortunately, the computer training of today continues to stress programming and history instead of how to *use* the microcomputer.

The emphasis on learning programming and history of computers as an instructional set stems from the time when little or no software existed for microcomputers. If the micro was to be used, the individual had to develop his or her own programs since none were available for purchase. This most often meant learning to program in BASIC

Introduction

(Beginners All-Purpose Symbolic Instruction Code) or even more complicated programming languages such as FORTRAN, COBOL and so on. Today it's a different story. There is a wide variety of commercially available software to choose from. "Basement" software developers and major publishers have provided a wide variety of educational and special applications software. True, it takes a little effort to find some of it (and not all of it is good), but there are reliable publications that review software both from a purpose and quality standpoint. Between print periodicals and computer data bases, access to current software information should be no problem. If someone wants to create their own courseware, there are skeleton programs called "authoring systems" ready to accept lesson materials just by learning a few simple directions and commands instead of complicated programming languages.

To be a microcomputer user is to use the machine and existing software to meet specific needs. From a technical point of view this means inserting the software, turning on the computer and following the directions given. To use peripheral devices you will have to learn to plug a few cables here and there, maybe even plug in a chip or two, but directions accompany these user modifications, or the device will tell you to "see your dealer" if the procedure is at all complicated. Users can now take full advantage of the computer software combination to complete a given task. It makes little difference what task the software is designed to achieve because the microcomputer will perform any task the software tells it to do. This makes the microcomputer a tool with thousands of uses, under direct control of the user.

The user concept allows anyone to reap the benefits of the computer. Age is no barrier nor is physical ability. There may be a problem of access for the physically handicapped but once the hardware and/or software interfaces have been established, the microcomputer is there for them as well. With today's technology, there is no reason computer access should not be available for everyone.

The material in this book covers the use of microcomputers in special education and the multitude of uses this technology offers the handicapped. All of what appears on these pages refers to user-oriented applications of the computer and requires no programming knowledge by the user. The information has been gathered as the result of the author being the parent of a handicapped child, a school district courseware developer, the publisher of a newspaper dealing with microcomputer usage by the handicapped, a computer workshop director and a computer *user*. I have not found it necessary to become a computer programmer nor do I expect to. The hardware and software exist to deliver educational and vocational benefits to the handicapped, just as they exist for all other people.

Microcomputer Resource Book
for
Special Education

Overview
1

Microcomputers can provide a solution to many problems facing the handicapped. Today, a microcomputer can bring speech to the nonvocal, telephone use to the deaf, grade II Braille or voice to the blind and environmental control to the physically handicapped. It can remove the paper and pencil blockade for the learning disabled and improve the quality of life for the mentally handicapped. All of these dramatic uses of the microcomputer can be accomplished without knowing one word of programming.

These and thousands of other uses of the microcomputer can be implemented just "using" the machine. The delivery of this information, to the people who can, is the focus of this book.

There is so much to offer through the implementation of the microcomputer; however, one barrier exists that must be overcome before universal usage by the handicapped can be a reality. This barrier is not cost, or lack of technology. It is an informational one.

Within my own small circle of friends and relatives, myths and misinformation still prevail, such as:

> The lady who says, "I can't use the microcomputer! I'm not a math major."

> The teacher who stands by watching the microcomputer/printer and says, "I'll never be able to write a program to do that!"

The man who refuses to even sit down at the micro because, as he puts it, "I'll erase everything the computer is doing if I push the wrong key."

The parent who insists, "This whole computer thing is way over my head. I'll never be able to understand how the kids do it."

A similar list of comments can be heard by anyone who bothers to survey a school or neighborhood. If the person is over twenty-five and has never used a computer, there is likely to be something mysterious and intimidating about these machines.

Through no great fault of its own, the public has been buffaloed by the intimidating aspects of large computers. There is the massive computer control room of NASA as viewed on television just before a space launch, or the image of giant mainframes spitting out credit card billings, all very impersonal and complicated. The prevailing view of such matters is "genius at work," portraying an environment foreign to mere mortals.

Along came the microcomputer, also called the *personal computer*, and the public reacted to the "computer" part with awe and bewilderment. Even though this new era of computing used a different language, BASIC (touted as a "user friendly language"), the public was unwilling or unable to come to terms with the idea of learning a new language just to communicate with a machine.

Hobbyists began to program and pursue their goals, in GOSUB and IF/THEN statements. They could produce the software to make the computer do what they wanted, but what of the general population? They stood by watching and wondering. The computer was everywhere but still about as impersonal and unfamiliar as the old style mainframes. When the only game in town was the huge mainframe, not being able to program was expected. Suddenly, the computer industry was telling the world "anyone can do this, . . . in just a few hours, you too can be a programmer."

Nothing could have been further from the truth and nothing more damaging to the actual use of the microcomputer as a tool. The rift continued to grow between those who could use the machine and those who could not. The effect of that rift made those unable to program uneasy, even downright afraid of using the software the programmers developed.

There were those in education who recognized the long-term value of the microcomputer in their field. However, most of them assumed that programming was the only way humans could gain access to the micro. It followed that everyone should learn to program.

The microcomputer industry flourished and a new industry emerged. Software, tons of it, was being created by a cottage industry of programmers. Soon major academic publishers joined the boom and *bang*, quality software to do just about anything was on the market.

Back in education, however, the momentum for teaching everyone to program was gathering. Buzz words like "computer literacy" and "CAI" (Computer Assisted Instruction) took over. The wheels were in motion. Educators braved the language barrier and began two major areas of computer usage in education. First, and still dominant, is the "Let's make everyone computer literate," a combination of history and/or programming, erroneously taught as the access to microcomputer usage. Second, there was the transformation of an old medium into the new box: take text from books and move it to the computer screen. Both are useful, but neither addresses the actual use of the microcomputer as a machine of varied uses to solve specific problems and neither explores the wealth of software that already has been written to allow the use of the microcomputer as a tool.

The microcomputer and existing software have the potential to make common computer usage a reality. Until the programming myths are laid to rest, however, the likelihood of effective implementation of this tool in education and for the handicapped is not very good.

In the early 1980s, the major obstacle was still software. Education's preoccupation with teaching programming resulted in a lack of awareness, much less use, of existent applicable software. This lack of awareness resulted in a total void of any comprehensive evaluation of software. There was no place to look except in the commercially produced software directories, wading through hundreds of listings to find one, maybe two, good programs in a sea of mediocre offerings. Part of this problem was attributable to the computer hobbyist attempting to create educational software but not knowing much about educational standards. The other was teachers, knowing a lot about education, but darn little about programming. The result—many useless hours of wheel spinning by both and a good many inappropriate programs sold as "microcomputer applications for education." It was hard to come away from software evaluation sessions without a sour taste in the mouth. Many educational computer pioneers were driven to near despair.

For those looking for special education applications, the situation was even worse. Nowhere was there even a partial listing of special-applications software. If you wanted to find something to serve the needs of the handicapped, you were at Ground Zero and nothing but a systematic search of all potentially useful software would solve the problem.

The software industry was growing with great speed, yet few educators were looking at what that industry was churning out to see if it was usable. Those in a position to evaluate the programs were often too busy trying to produce their own software.

It wasn't that software didn't exist. In fact, it might be said that too much existed, with no way to distinguish the good from the bad, short of running every program.

It didn't take long before attempts were made to start weeding out the collection. Magazines directed to educators began reviewing software. For those interested, it was possible to get some idea of what certain programs were like before buying. However, the vast majority of programs were simply listed in an ever growing number of "software directories" with mere existence the only criterion for listing.

Adding to the difficulty of finding appropriate special-education programs was the nonlisted software. This was most often the case with special applications programs. Viewed as having limited appeal, these programs were very often not submitted to the directory publishers because their producers were solving an individual's problem and once that problem was solved, the software went on the shelf, never reaching production or marketing to the public.

With all this confusion about software, it is understandable why so few people were willing to pursue microcomputer use applications for the handicapped. Discovering appropriate educational software was a monumental task in itself. Locating special-education applications took Herculean effort and dedication.

Today, some of these problems still remain, but the situation has gotten much better. More and better software review systems are in place. Many periodicals exist that regularly review software in great detail. On-line data base systems that specialize in evaluation of educational software now are available. However, their contribution to the dissemination of information is limited to those with the special equipment that allows computer-to-computer access over telephone lines.

Another development that has improved software information is that major publishers and distributors have come on the scene. Through their efforts, large collections of high-quality software are much easier to identify than before. Many of these companies have begun their own software search and development divisions and the result is a continually growing library of quality software to choose from. "Where to find software" is largely a question of the past. However, it still leaves the question of "what software is applicable" up to the individual buyer.

There still are problems within the software and educational communities that make implementation of the microcomputer in special education difficult. These problems center around software information getting to the people who can use it and identifying what software is actually appropriate for use. The first of those problems will not be solved until there is more organized access to pertinent information about handicapped usage and more people become familiar with microcomputer applications. The second, however, can be solved by following simple rules that address the software availability that exists and putting that software to work. Software availability is expanding daily. In a field with such rapid expansion, what is unavailable today may exist tenfold tomorrow. But once the general rules are understood and put to use, the new additions will simply enhance the existent usage.

General Rules To Finding Software

Software, that elusive part of the equation, is there—it's just a matter of finding it. As has been pointed out, there is little software listed as "special education software." This does not mean that none exists. It just means that the software industry has not addressed or understood the special education uses for its products. To solve this problem, identify the "need" and look for software to fill that need. If the child is twelve years old and in the sixth grade but having problems with math facts at the third grade level, there are hundreds of useful tutorial math programs that could be used. Most educational software is listed by grade level, thereby making the identification of special education applications a simple matter once the need has been determined.

The objective of "finding software" is best obtained by following Rule 1.

RULE 1	Software does not have to say "handicapped" on the label to be useful in special education.

The special education uses of the microcomputer are endless, especially if you take the labels off the software and apply what the programs do for the needs of the child. Take, for example, typing tutors. Traditionally typing is taught in the high schools. It has been thought of as training for those students headed for business careers. A far more realistic approach is to introduce typing skills in the elementary grades, via a typing tutor and a microcomputer. The reasons are obvious. First, these children will be expected to interact with microcomputers throughout their lives. The most efficient method of interaction now available is through the typewriter-style keyboard. Training for these children should include typing, the most effective method of access to the very tool that can help them. This matching of software to need, though akin to Rule 1, develops into Rule 2.

RULE 2   Train handicapped children to use the microcomputer as efficiently as possible, as early as possible.

A teacher of learning disabled students put it very well when he said, "There is a lot of tedium in this business." Over and over again, repeat, repeat and repeat, again and again. For most learning disabled children, regardless of the disability, learning must include a very tedious repetition of information. This tedium, for both teacher and child, can stifle motivation. It can produce angry emotional outbursts from student and teacher alike. One-on-one tutoring of facts, drill and practice, repeating over and over again, is ideally suited for the microcomputer. First, it is an unemotional device that operates at the speed of the student. Second, the microcomputer is nonjudgmental except in its ability to choose correct or incorrect responses, thereby allowing the student hundreds of attempts without embarrassment or stigma attached to the repetition process. Third, it frees the teacher for more creative activities during one-on-one human encounters with the students. Fourth, children are far more motivated when the drill and practice is done on a microcomputer. As one teacher put it, "We couldn't get them to do these exercises at all, willingly. Now, we can't tear them away when the same material is on the microcomputer." This leads to Rule 3.

RULE 3   The microcomputer can provide motivating drill-and-practice for handicapped children.

Individual educational needs of the handicapped child have been recognized and served for a very long time. Each child is different and each has needs that are difficult and time consuming to serve. One-on-one teacher time, dedicated to serving those needs, has been the only way to bring the necessary help to these children—that is, until the advent of the microcomputer and programs called authoring systems. With authoring systems, it is possible to create specific courseware (learning materials used on microcomputers) tailored exactly to the need of each child, and you don't have to be a programmer to do it!

Authoring systems are tools. They are programs or procedural languages written as a skeleton to which instructional materials must be added. This skeleton is "bug free" and simply requires the addition of the desired lesson material to turn it into individualized courseware. The courseware prepared by authoring systems can offer a cost effective alternative to the one-on-one teacher tutorial. Both drill-and-practice and concept reinforcement can be presented by microcomputer, not once during class time, but again and again, at home as well as in the educational environment. For the first time a tutorial package of motivating, stimulating materials can go with the child, to his or her environment, for as long as is necessary. For these and many other reasons discussed in later chapters, authoring systems are the base for Rule 4.

RULE 4   Educational use of the microcomputer for handicapped children should include individual courseware prepared with authoring systems.

Rules 1 through 4 deal with the microcomputer as an extension of the teacher or parent in the areas of tutorial needs. In this role the computer becomes as close to a one-on-one human encounter as is possible, without it actually being another human being. But this is also an extension of the "right or wrong," "black or white" side of education. Granted, it is a necessary side and the microcomputer meets those needs very well. However, this same microcomputer can become a tool on another side of education which is equally, if not more important. I often refer to this as "the need to release the caged intellect of the handicapped child."

Thinking and problem solving skills, which will allow a child to reason for himself, are very often neglected in the education of the handicapped. This often is the case because there is limited time and most of that time must be spent attempting to close the learning gap created by the handicap. There is a tendency to stress the acquisition of facts, the "right and wrong" side, because these elements appear to be necessary for survival.

As a tool to develop self-expression and reasoning skills, the microcomputer can play perhaps its most important role in aiding the handicapped child. By putting the child in charge of the microcomputer with a language like Logo, there can be a role reversal that makes the child the teacher. There is great truth in the old adage, "We learn by doing," and with Logo, the doing is original, yet the child is working with facts to accomplish his or her inventive creation. The child deals with elements of reality and is in charge of their organization, allowing for the creativity within the child to develop. In problem solving, building an organizational structure, uninhibited by the concepts of right or wrong, the child can explore his or her own ability to reason without an imposed pattern or instructional set.

Much the same effect can be achieved, in theory at least, with any computer programming. However, computer languages have made it impossible to implement this concept with children—until the creation of Logo. Logo is a children's language, yet a very powerful computer language. Its multitude of uses as a developmental tool for handicapped children is discussed in later chapters and is the basis for Rule 5.

RULE 5   Microcomputer usage for handicapped children should include intellect expansion through the use of Logo.

These rules are offered as guidelines, a first step toward bringing microcomputer technology to special education and to at-home use of the microcomputer for handicapped children. They represent a strong beginning for any parent or educator who wants to use this technology to educate and improve the quality of life of these children. They do not, however, begin to explore the full impact of microcomputer technology for the handicapped.

Within the chapters of this book, the scope of potential use and service these machines can bring to the handicapped population will be discussed. It should be stressed that what is included in these pages are user-oriented applications, available for anyone to use. Using commercially available programs, no microcomputer programming knowledge is required to implement any of the applications nor is any extensive technical expertise required to plug in the software, microcomputer and peripheral combinations necessary. All that is required is the desire to use existing technology to meet normal needs and improve the quality of life for people.

Communication

One of the greatest attributes of the microcomputer is its versatility. Just about any information can be "digitized" (reduced to computer readable data consisting of the binary numbers 0 and 1), then reconstructed or reformulated and presented to a user. An example is the language we use. The microcomputer digitizes the alpha/numeric symbols of language in order to work with it. The power of the microcomputer comes into play when it is used in conjunction with peripherals. The peripherals added to the microcomputer result in translating devices that can use different output modes such as text to the screen, language through speech synthesizers, printers, etc.

One of these many different output modes is audible tone signals achieved through the addition of a modem or acoustical coupler. This configuration of equipment allows the digitized language of the microcomputer to be converted to tones and transmitted over telephone lines. Modems and acoustical couplers transform the microcomputer into a telecommunications device, opening up the ability to send and receive written communication over the telephone.

My husband and I had a personal interest in this form of communication because of our profoundly deaf son, Marc. As a deaf member within a hearing society, Marc was limited to personal communications of either face-to-face voice communication, via his ability to lip read, or written notation, either direct to the recipient or for longer distance via the U. S. mail. As a teenager of thirteen, his need (let alone desire) for extended communication ability was a "normal" need, yet it was out of reach because of his handicap.

The Telecommunications Devices for the Deaf (TDDs) were the only alternative to deaf isolation until July of 1981, when my husband, Budd, asked American Telephone and Telegraph Corporation to change its policy and include microcomputers as Telecommunications Devices for the Deaf. The resulting rule change made microcomputers eligible for the same toll rate reductions that had previously been restricted only to traditional TDD usage. The dramatic effect of that rule change and the impending impact on the speech and hearing handicapped individual's ability to communicate with the rest of the world is discussed in Chapters III and V.

As a communications device, the microcomputer will have a universal impact on the acquisition and dissemination of information. Electronic editions of the daily newspaper, convenience shopping, banking, personal communications via electronic mail, access to college campuses full of information such as medical or law libraries, etc., will affect the lives of anyone living in the computer age. For the first time, the handicapped will have equal access to that information. This will give them an equality of opportunity never before available. The blind will never be restricted to someone else's choice of literature, the hearing impaired will be able to communicate with anyone over great distances, and the physically handicapped will have access to any information they choose from their wheelchair. Telecommunications via the microcomputer will, for the first time, give the handicapped equal opportunity in society. Understanding that all of this is possible today, and to know that in most instances it is not being implemented, should concern a great many people. The reality is that few understand that it is possible today, and until this is understood, a vast resource of humanity is forced to assume the role of society's liability rather than its rightful role as an asset. Without this technology the majority of handicapped persons are trapped, unable to assume fruitful and productive roles in society.

Environmental Control

There is a catch-all word that is used to describe the population with special needs. That word is *handicapped.* I use the word even though I'm sure I dislike it more than most. I use the word because it is understood to mean "different" and to that end these people do have some "different" needs. But these people also have the same needs as everyone else. Regardless of what part of nature has failed them or what the hand of fate has dealt them, they are members of society. Their normal needs should be considered and the tools that can meet their normal needs provided. We live in a time when great progress has been made to provide the tools to meet those needs.

In a world where the environment for a given situation can be modified to meet that situation, we have the opportunity to enhance the quality of life for many people. The microcomputer offers the ability to modify any number of environments an endless number of ways.

EDUCATIONAL

The educational environment is changing as a result of the microcomputer and will continue to change. There is the opportunity to deliver educational needs on a much more individualized basis to all children. The need for individualized learning materials for the handicapped has been recognized for a very long time and the creation of Public Law 94-142 is a visible sign of this recognition. Now we have the opportunity to incorporate new tools to help meet that individualized need. The microcomputer can be used to create an educational environment suited exactly to the needs of the child.

One of the biggest constraints forbidding this individualized attention in the past has been money to provide one-on-one human services. Now we have a tool perfectly suited to interact with the child's needs and provide these one-on-one services at modest cost, wiping away any excuse for less than individual education plans.

Educators can now produce a wide range of services that were out of reach before the microcomputer. A gifted blind child can receive the volumes of text required for learning. Autistic children can have companions capable of continuous repetitive behavior to match their own, yet able to respond instantaneously to a change of behavior when change occurs.

In my desire to point out the power of the microcomputer I often forget to acknowledge its limitations. A computer cannot love. It cannot replace a warm smile or a cuddle. This device is just a tool to add to the overall delivery system of education. To that end, it can also be viewed as a tool that can bring smiles to a lot of little faces in great need of a reason to smile—an environmental change worth the effort in many cases.

PHYSICAL

Another area of environmental control adaptable by the computer is the physical. To brew the coffee at a set time or to provide control of the apparatus needed for a paralyzed muscle to regenerate itself is accomplished by the same tool. The flexibility of this machine and the endless services that it can provide to change the physical environment of the handicapped staggers the imagination.

Tasks as simple as turning on lights, controlling temperature, raising and lowering a bed, or opening the door can be controlled by a microcomputer and, at the same time, it can control the movements of a wheelchair. Almost all of the physical environmental requirements of a handicapped individual can be met with the aid of a microcomputer.

For efficient control of the physical environment there must be functional control of the microcomputer. The severely physically disabled may require vocal-input devices that allow voice control over the functions of the computer. For the nonvocal this can be eye switches or any number of various switch configurations that can be activated by any reliable muscle. In gaining functional control of the microcomputer, the individual gains the ability to be in actual control of his or her environment.

The microcomputer also allows the handicapped individual to use the device for more common tasks. Word processing, education and entertainment are now within the reach of this individual through the same device that meets the special needs he or she may have.

Microcomputer technology will influence everyone. Putting the disabled back in charge of their own environments makes this tool even more exciting for them than for the rest of society. For the disabled, the microcomputer truly will bring a revolution.

Another way to look at a microcomputer is as a mini-environment of its own. From the comfort of your home this device can be a Spanish tutor, a video game tournament, and a bookkeeper all in the same day, in the same hour if you are good at Spanish. It will be anything you want it to be, on your time schedule and on your terms. With this kind of flexibility any environment you choose can be entered and explored under your control. This is a far cry from just a few short years ago when this kind of specialization of purpose meant investment in as many tools as specialities. Today it is one—one tool to serve the many needs of man.

Future

In the future the handicapped will still have special needs, much the same as today. Stopping short of a medical miracle, our son will be deaf for the rest of his life. We cannot change the disability, only the way he can deal with it. This is true with most disabled children and adults.

What is important is that these people must be provided with the tools that will make the disabilities less able to rob them of their normal needs.

Looking at the microcomputer of today as one of these tools will improve the outlook dramatically. If we take what is available today and assume further advances, the future looks even brighter.

A child with cerebral palsy sits in a wheelchair, unable to communicate, yet the knowledge to bring him communication exists. Today, it would be possible to give communication to this child through speech synthesis and word processing. This was the case with a young man in southern Minnesota. His teacher wrote of the future for his student, "He now has the potential to converse with anyone he wishes. The future holds the never-before possibility to do such things as write his autobiography, or to talk to a person thousands of miles away via his computerized voice . . ."

The job in the future is to see that this happens for all such disabled. There is no longer a technological or cost barrier, just an informational one. The future for the disabled, and their use of these new tools, rests largely on spreading the word and becoming a computer user. The faster that job is done, the faster this technology will get to the people who need it.

THE REAL FUTURE

The real future lies with the potential for productivity within the handicapped population. Given the tools, these people have a sincere contribution to make toward their own destiny and that of society. The handicapped want to work. They want to be independent. Now they have realistic hope.

The future will be a place where the movement-handicapped, those afflicted with neuromuscular or neurological disorders, will be as much as part of the work force as they would like to be. The work force will probably include as many folks who are willfully home-bound as those who must be. Banks, major corporations, small businesses, even factories will employ many of their personnel from their homes via computer terminals.

A blind individual will have access to reading machines, but instead of prohibitively expensive designs, this can be done via microcomputers and a voice synthesizer that will convert any text file to speech. Conversion of the output from a microcomputer to Braille is another choice available. This newly acquired ability to gain access to communication will help the blind erase a major obstacle in their path to productivity. Surely their quality of life and feeling of self-worth will be significantly enhanced with these tools.

There is reason to believe that these enhancements of life and productivity via the microcomputer will affect *all* persons with handicaps. The physically handicapped, the blind, the deaf, the mentally retarded, the learning disabled, all will be able to take advantage of the growth in this technology. It will influence the day-to-day experience of adults, but perhaps more importantly it will influence the education and development of the children.

I can't help but think of the learning disabled boy whose pen flows across paper, recalling from memory a picture he saw months before. There, on the paper is a perfect duplicate of the picture. Every element in flawless detail. Yet, this child is diagnosed (classified) as "learning disabled" because he cannot read. What untapped ability does this child have—to recall pictures, images from his memory, yet unable to learn how to read by current teaching methods. I see the microcomputer as a tool that could lead us to the understanding of such mysteries.

As you make your way through the chapters in this book, remember that the microcomputer is just a tool, a means to an end. That end may be different for the deaf child than for the blind child in terms of how they will use the microcomputer to reach their goal. The add-on hardware may be different, the software may be different, but it is still the same tool.

Learning about this tool, reading about its applications, will certainly help motivate you but to use it, just *use* it. Microcomputers are like cars; you don't learn to drive one by reading about it, but you don't have to know how to overhaul the engine either. In spite of what most current "computer literacy" courses suggest, you do not have to learn a programming language to operate a microcomputer. You do have to learn how to use the accelerator, the clutch and the brake, so to speak. You will have to become familiar with the kinds of software and peripherals needed to meet a particular goal. It will take more than a ten minute test drive watching someone else to get started, but so does driving a car. Plan for a good two-day hands-on *user* workshop to get you started. Then with the experience that comes with use, you will be able to use this machine effectively to fill your needs.

Hints For Implementation
II

The major question today is, "How will microcomputer technology reach the handicapped?" Some common element must take the responsibility of introduction, training and implementation of this tool. The educational system seems the most appropriate for several reasons. The most obvious, of course, is the placement of all children into the system, the common denominator, if you will. Second is the reality that microcomputers will make the job of education easier and more complete. Because this tool has so much to offer as a teaching device, its placement as a tool in the educational system seems assured. The crucial element is to make sure the training and use extend beyond drill-and-practice Computer Assisted Instruction (CAI) concepts to the long-term impact microcomputers will have on society as a life style.

    The microcomputer offers the ability to remove the "result" of many disabilities. The microcomputer and modem, as a communications device, should be part of every speech and hearing impaired child's training. With it the child will learn how to extend his or her communication skills into the hearing world. Without it, a major use of the microcomputer is ignored. To teach a nonvocal child to read and then to stop short of giving him the synthesized voice to tell about what he read is cheating him out of what technology can do to remove the result of the disability. These added uses and concepts of the microcomputer should be included in the special education delivery system.

The key elements of microcomputer implementation for a handicapped child are using software and hardware that gives:

1. access,
2. motivation,
3. authoring systems,
4. self-expression (Logo) and
5. normal function.

All of these elements exist and can be used by special education professionals or parents who are willing to take the time to learn about microcomputer use. There is nothing mysterious or difficult in applying microcomputer technology. It is a question of knowing what can be done, where to find the elements and how to put them together.

Access becomes the single most important element of implementation, because without it the student is unable to use the microcomputer.

The most common access method, the keyboard, is configured like a typical typewriter with several additional special function keys and in some instances, a numerical key pad. For children able to use the standard keyboard, typing tutor software should be introduced as early as possible. Developing typing skills will enhance the efficiency with which children can use the microcomputer during the educational years and will give them a valuable skill that can be used throughout their lives.

Typing tutors are programs available for all popular microcomputer brands. The tutors are self-paced typing drills that most often are menu-select. The menus offer choices of drill, from individual letter and numeral practice to paragraphs that are constructed (by the computer) from the most recent letter practice. Each drill is timed, with a word-per-minute readout after each lesson. Some will indicate the keys on which the user needs more practice by indicating the keys used most inefficiently. Others have lesson management capabilities where records of the student's performance during practice are automatically entered for later review by teacher or parent.

For very young children, or for kids needing a motivational boost, typing tutors also come in game formats. These are excellent for letter recognition as well as keyboard skills. The fact that they are presented to the users as games that offer entertaining and motivating activities enhances their use as skill development tools.

Access through the keyboard can be achieved without standard typing ability, however. Simple keyguards that cover the standard keyboards can be installed for mouthstick, handprod or headpointer typists. These keyguards can also improve accuracy for typists with spasticity or other coordination difficulties. One such keyboard for the

Apple is designed with ⅝ inch keyhole diameters (with ¾ inch between keys) making accuracy much easier and stick typing a controllable reality.

Another access method has been developed through a game control modification. Since the game controllers are switches that send signals to the computer, an extension of wires connected to any other manageable switch does the same thing, send a signal to the computer. This could be an eye switch, a foot control, or any single switch that can be activated by the user with any reliable muscle control. This form of access demands modified programs that scan the options available on the screen and allows a choice to be made by activating a single switch.

Other types of switches can be plugged directly into the microcomputer's game control socket, offering control of the microcomputer without any direct keyboard interaction. These access devices can give complete control of the computer when appropriate switches are matched with the users. Breath, contact, or any other switch that can be reliably controlled by the user becomes the contact point between user and microcomputer. There can be single or multiple switch interfaces depending on the mobility of the user.

Software has been written to support single and multiple switch access that provides everything from motor training games (for beginning use to develop the necessary muscle control) to single switch typewriter programs. One example is Handicapped Typewriter. It takes an Apple II, printer, modem and loudspeaking telephone and turns them into a single switch communications and environmental control system. The combination provides a picture of a keyboard on the television screen; characters are selected by the control of a scanning cursor. Also included is a user definable word and phrase dictionary, a calculator, a telephone answering, dialing and directory service and an environmental control system—all under control of a simple, single switch closure.

Switch adapters can effectively provide access for severely physically handicapped and nonvocal individuals. A modification can be made to the game controls by a do-it-yourself method of hooking wires to the leads inside the controls to your choice of switch. This modification is inexpensive and simple to do for single switch control. More sophisticated, multi-switch controls, though very easy to install (a simple plug-in pin connector), are more complex in design and can be purchased from suppliers who specialize in adaptive hardware modifications. A list of hardware modification manufacturers is listed in Appendix G. Where possible, a brief description regarding the kinds of modifications available is also included.

Keyboard emulators or software, designed for single or multi-switch interaction with the microcomputer and assorted peripherals, can give profoundly motor-handicapped and nonverbal individuals access to speech through voice synthesis, a printer for written communications, many educational applications and complete environmental control. These kinds of software and hardware are discussed in greater detail in Chapter III under the subheading "Physically Handicapped," and a list of suppliers and publishers of specialty software is included in Appendix B.

Another type of access to the microcomputer is voice entry. Here, though the technology is relatively new, a long list of applications for the handicapped is emerging. Systems of voice entry can give total control of the microcomputer by voice command only. The systems can be trained to recognize *any* voice. They can be made to do *any* computer functions, just as keyboard access would. The need for formal language, as such, is not required because the systems can be trained to recognize any reliably repeatable group of sounds as access commands. It does not take long before a long list of applications for the handicapped come to mind.

There are other access methods such as touch-screens (activating the computer by touching the monitor screen) and light pens (a small light source that activates the computer when light contact is made with the screen).

The access method used will depend on the needs of the individual child but one thing should be made clear: Access to the microcomputer can be accomplished, regardless of the handicap and with very little additional expense. Many of the hardware modifications can be purchased for between $10 and $100. Even complete voice entry can be added for under $1,000. Software, then, becomes the other expense. Programs of even the most specialized nature are available from $10 to $300 with very few over that figure. These costs are comparable with other applications of software offered to education, business and industry. Only in rare instances is specialty hardware or software priced out of line with these standards.

Many special applications programs are available for the cost of reproduction—in other words, free. These usually are the result of federal or state grant programs that underwrite the cost of developing specific software for the handicapped. By law, these programs are available to the public at minimal charge, usually the cost of duplication and documentation, without profit.

Once access to the microcomputer has been accomplished, the motivational, educational and vocational potential of the machine can be addressed.

Motivation

While interviewing a teacher for a newspaper story on a junior high school learning disabled program, I was told, "If the microcomputer could do nothing else, it would be worth it just for the motivation it gives these kids." The teacher was standing by the Apple II microcomputer placed on a small table near a window. He reached into a box and handed me seven diskettes. "These are my treats," he said. "I used to spend my own money to come up with trinkets, rewards, that I could use with the students, but I haven't bought any in two years. The microcomputer has replaced those."

The diskettes were games. Most of them were arcade-style, shoot-em-up entertainment. On completion of an assignment or for doing well on the day's work, the student was given ten minutes at the end of the hour with the disk of his or her choice as pure recreation. This was a controlled tutorial classroom with only one or two students in any given hour, but somehow everyone participating in the learning disabled program knew if computer time had been given as a reward, what game had been played, and what the high score was. A contest had developed that served the teacher's motivational goals very well.

A high school hearing impaired program demonstrated another example of games put to good use. Here the students could earn "Computer Bucks" for any number of goal-oriented achievements, each worth ten minutes of recreational computer time. Students could spend their rewards during lunch periods or other free time. Needless to say, lunch periods turned into computer room free-for-alls, in hot competition of the championship.

I am certainly in no position to analyze why computer games are so popular with children, but I don't think it's necessary to understand why in order to use the result. They are popular, and it seems practical to use the motivation they instill to further educational goals.

Games make an excellent introduction to the use of the microcomputer with children and adults alike. With kids, there is rarely a problem in getting them to interact with the keyboard; they seem to jump right in and take over. With adults, however, the situation is much different. Teachers and parents are very often timid about sitting down to the keyboard and actually doing something with the computer. There seem to be all sorts of fears and misinformation about the microcomputer stored within them that makes them say things like, "If I hit the wrong key, won't I erase everything the computer is doing?" or "I'm sure I can't operate a computer, I don't have a math background."

To counter the inherent fears of the unknown that adults have about microcomputers, start them with the very games that are popular with the kids. The game format seems to dissolve the fear of the keyboard. Before you know it, the mysteries that surround the machine are dislodged and the perspective of "tool" or "means to an end" comes into focus.

Games and game formats for learning have always been used to provide variety and motivation in the educational process. However, the microcomputer offers a new dimension to this concept.

A game as old as Hangman has a new luster when an animated "smiley face" is added to the correct answer. It's still Hangman, with all the spelling drill that was there with pencil and paper, but instead of two people playing, it is available with one person and the computer. The software can be modified to include any list of words. The child is guided through the game with positive reinforcement and an interaction that has the spirit of competition without the negatives that can sometimes come with human encounter—an enhanced version of an old game, made better by the microcomputer.

Tic-Tac-Toe is another example of the old transformed by the microcomputer. A wonderful problem solving skill development program has been created around the game of Tic-Tac-Toe. Instead of winning as the object of the game, the program is designed to teach a child how to predict who will win the game. Again, what formerly required two players is reduced to one and the resulting interaction between the microcomputer and the child provides an endless, tireless companion to skill development.

It is not an exaggeration to say there are thousands of educational games for microcomputers on the market. Everything from the simple Hangman to complex simulation games to playing detective is available. All of them have something to teach or reinforce in the student, but it is the motivational element that these games provide that makes them such an important part of education of the handicapped. If the tedium can become less negative, if the child wants to learn, a good share of the battle is won.

A subtle but real part of motivation is how the child really feels about himself. It is very hard to keep an image of self-worth when the environment of learning is always negative. The authoritative figure is always saying, "Do it again," or "No, Johnny, this way." There is a limit to the amount of implied failure a child can deal with before motivation suffers.

With my son, the implied failure caused by needed repetition of language was a constant problem. We struggled for years to keep his image of himself sound, to keep faith in himself and others who were trying to help him. He found the "Do it again," "Say it again," a constant reminder of his inability to perform the way they wanted him to. It was very hard to keep him motivated and to hold his desire to interact with others when he was conditioned to expect correction or even rejection of his response.

When he was thirteen years old the limit of his tolerance was reached. Over a three month period a slow but steady erosion of his self-image resulted in almost total loss of motivation for learning. It finally came down to his total rejection of school and any desire to continue trying.

Our answer to Marc's problem was the microcomputer. With just the suggestion that he could use the microcomputer for drill and practice, a willingness to "try again" returned. Within a month, a revitalized desire to learn developed. He wanted more and more vocabulary words to practice, more and more information on the computer to help him understand the concepts being taught in the classroom. After one year of computer usage, both at home and in school, Marc was asked to write a story about microcomputers and how he felt about using them in school. Here is his story.

> *My name is Marcus Hagen and I am 13 years old. Last year I was in the 7th grade at Belle Plaine Junior High, in Belle Plaine, Minnesota.*
>
> *The seventh grade was very hard for me in social studies and science. I could not understand the books and sometimes I could not lip read the teacher. It was so bad that I did not want to go to school at all.*
>
> *My mother learned about computers and asked the school to try Computer Assisted Instruction for me. They said yes, so my mother started writing programs for me to use at school.*
>
> *Things got better right away. The computer helps me learn new words and meanings.*
>
> *I used the computer at least 2 hours a day at school. I am learning to type with a computer typing tutor and I am writing this story with a word processing system.*
>
> *My mother is writing courseware in science and geography for next year for me and other eighth graders.*
>
> *I like computers because they help me learn. I wish all handicapped people could use computers because if they could, it would make life easier for them.*
>
> *You can use a microcomputer to learn, for typing, for word processing, for games or just about anything. You can even use it as a TDD now that the telephone company said it is okay to use the microcomputer as a telecommunication device for the deaf.*
>
> *Sometime it is hard for me to understand the teachers because they talk very fast. When they talk fast they asked*

> me, "what does that word mean." I said it all wrong. I felt so embarrassed because my class laughed at me. When I use the computer, the class didn't laugh. The computer does not make fun of me, it just teaches me.

There is much to learn from Marc's words. He is giving us a look into the world of implied inferiority. He is telling us that the computer gives him a chance to be himself, to learn without ridicule. He has an understanding of the computer's contribution to the way people view him. In his opinion, the computer protects his self-image and to him, that is important. To me, his mother, it is crucial.

Our observations and those of Marc's teachers have shown that the computer provided Marc with a motivational spark. He was able to learn from a tool that did not laugh at him and that was a new beginning. The learning gave him confidence in himself and allowed him to move ahead into the world of computer usage to meet his everyday needs.

As a motivational tool, the microcomputer is a very important device. It is much more than a reward system or entertainment center for pleasure. It is a real companion to learning in a new environment. The need for a new environment, at least in Marc's case, was very real. If the microcomputer can produce an atmosphere less threatening and thereby more conducive to learning, then let's use it.

Marc's story is not unusual. Hundreds of stories like his have been told by teachers using microcomputers with the handicapped. If there is a lesson to be learned from this, it is that there is a need to explore the environments used for learning and incorporate the microcomputer as a tool to preserve the self-image of these children before they lose their motivation for learning.

Of course, the challenge is to get the microcomputer into the hands of these children. To do this, the microcomputer must be understood to be a tool. Just as the pencil and paper, the motion picture projector or the tape recorder are tools, so is the computer.

Individual Needs Met by Software

Software is the key to use of the microcomputer. With appropriate software, the micro can be anything you would like it to be. Without it, the machine is useless.

Today, much of the educational software designed for popular microcomputer brands is "brand specific," which means that which runs on one brand is not compatible with other brands. An Atari diskette will not run on an Apple and vice versa. This problem of incompatibility of software presents some significant problems for schools as well as parents.

In schools, it often forces administrative decisions making a school district "brand specific" because of former hardware purchases regardless of what software/hardware combination would best meet a specific need. The district cannot justify supporting two completely different hardware and software investments so they stay with the brand first purchased in order to protect the original investment.

Good advice to teachers and parents, alike, is to determine the need, find the software to fill that need, and let the software determine the brand of computer to buy. This may sound like strange advice, but the computer is nothing without the software. Unless you are a programmer and can write the necessary programs to meet your needs, it is necessary to determine the availability of software for a particular brand before you buy. Otherwise you will have a machine but you can't make it do what you want it to do.

In the educational area, six major brands have gained popularity and, from a software point of view, materials to meet most of the mainstream educational needs have been developed for all six brands. It is in the area of special applications software that caution is advised. If you have a need for a word processing program that converts text to grade II Braille and it is only available for one brand of microcomputer, your need pretty well dictates what brand of microcomputer you will buy.

Some software publishers make their products available in different flavors, publishing a popular program in several versions—an Apple disk, an Atari disk, a PET version, etc. When this is the case, and the software in question is exactly what you are looking for, it is possible to look at other considerations for the purchase of the micro brand, such as expandability or price.

Finding appropriate software for current or expanding needs is another question. Software is very hard to find if you are looking in a catalog under "Special Education." Here is an example found in one catalog. Forty-four pages of Apple specific educational software are listed. There is a section called "Special Education" but in it are only four pages, eight programs, all dealing with survival skills. The balance of the catalog is filled with excellent software selections dealing with math, science, social studies, language arts, etc. The problem is that some people would ignore the other forty pages of material. What is even more of a problem is that some of the most useful software, like word processing programs, was not listed in the educational section at all. They were listed under "Administrative Management." The answer is to assess the need and to look for software to fill the need, forgetting about the label or the source.

Sources of commercial software grow each day. It becomes a major task just to keep abreast of the new releases in general terms, much less to study them in any detail. One of the best ways to follow what's new in the software development field is to rely on the journals and magazines that specialize in software reviews. The reviews should tell you the subject of the material, grade level, what kind of computer the software is designed for, where the software can be obtained and how much it costs. In addition to this list, the review should tell you a bit about the program itself, how well the program meets the advertised goals, the quality of the information presented, its strengths and weaknesses, instructional usefulness, potential applications and overall educational value. The reviews should give enough information so that the reader can decide if the program merits further investigation.

Sometimes it's very hard to get a first-hand look at commercial software before buying, yet people want to know what the program actually does before committing funds for the purchase. Some publishers have solved this problem by having demonstration disks that show excerpts from the programs they offer. Others set up regional offices where software can be evaluated before purchase. Still others select distributors who regularly do business with the educational systems so that the software can be shown to teachers by the distributor. But there still are large amounts of educational software that are not handled in this fashion, making it very hard to get a first-hand look before purchase. In these cases, it can be useful to request a copy of the documentation for review. Certainly this is not as good as examining the program, but better than nothing.

Another way to investigate educational software is through computer data base. Anyone with a microcomputer and a modem can access (for a fee) large on-line services that specialize in listing and evaluating educational software. These systems provide search capabilities so that the user can find software, by subject, and get the pertinent information about a specific program much like a print review.

One of the best ways to get information about a program is to find someone who has actually used it. Talk to friends, or post a request for information on a computer bulletin board. Bulletin boards spring up around specific brands of microcomputers and many times around special interests. As user groups, these people share information readily and can be an invaluable resource for information to the new computer user.

AUTHORING SYSTEMS

Within the commercial software available to meet the needs of special education, one variety stands out above all the rest. This is software that allows computer courseware development without programming knowledge—authoring systems.

Authoring systems break down into two categories. First are mini authoring systems. These software selections allow creation of drill-and-practice lessons. The author (teacher or parent) can develop question/answer types of drills, including multiple choice, true and false, spelling, and even game formats like Hangman or word finds. The second type is major authoring systems. This is software that allows interactive courseware. The author can tell not only students when they are wrong, but also why they are wrong. These programs allow for the teaching of concepts as well as drill and practice.

Both types of authoring systems are available for all the major brands of microcomputers but can differ dramatically in ease of use and the power of the program itself.

Mini Authoring Systems

Many different kinds of mini authoring systems are available. Some are designed for word lists on the screen. Others have a printer routine built in so the word lists, or games generated from the word lists, can be printed for paper and pencil use. Some programs are question/answer formats with no word list capability. Still others combine both capabilities plus the print option in one program. The trick is to find a versatile program for your brand of micro.

Drill-and-practice authoring systems will probably become as much of a standard in education as "Dick and Jane," or "Run, Spot, run." The wide range of uses these systems have, and the fact that their content can be changed at will, make them invaluable. They can become a major part of the software used in meeting the needs of a child in special education.

A typical education plan can start with programs such as *Micro Quest* and *Vocab*. Both of these programs are part of a package of vocabulary facilities produced by TIES (Total Information Educational Systems) and are copyrighted by the Minnesota School Districts Data Processing Joint Board.

Both *Micro Quest* and *Vocab* are managed by the same teacher utilities disk. Each has a separate student presentation disk, *Micro Quest* for the question/answer and *Vocab* for word list activities.

Many learning disabled, speech and hearing handicapped students have problems in mainstream education centering around language deficiency. The ability to understand new vocabulary is directly proportional to the time available to introduce the vocabulary, to explain the meaning, and to devise a method of repeated usage so the child can retain the word. When I say "time available," I'm referring not only to teacher time for tutorial and parent time for reinforcement, but the time (and patience) of the child to tolerate enough one-on-one communication to get the job done. There usually is not enough "time" or "tolerance" available using traditional methods.

I would like to share some of the early, first-hand experiences and part of what was learned while planning and implementing a microcomputer applications program for our son.

The procedure was simple, once we discovered *Micro Quest* and *Vocab*. The first thing was to read the text of the social studies and science assignment to discover what words were going to present problems. At first, this was as high as 50 percent of the text. Next, I sat down at the microcomputer and wrote meanings for those words, at the appropriate language level, using the *Micro Quest* authoring system. I found myself posing question such as, "Which word means 'outside layer of the cell'" and offering multiple choices of "book, table, bed, and membrane" just to insure success. It also provided an uncomplicated method of introducing the new word. The next step was preparing a lesson with more challenge, using the new vocabulary word in the question and offering known vocabulary and new words in the answers. The third stage was actually integrating the language levels of the text into the questions and answers, thereby bringing Marc's comprehension of the new vocabulary up to his grade level.

The *Vocab* portion of this software package was used to generate word lists containing the new vocabulary. The program offers four screen game formats for further reinforcement: Hangman, Scramble, Spell1 and Spell2. The software also supports a wordmaze feature which allows puzzle sheets to be generated on the printer. This option not only generates a wordmaze of any size up to thirty characters but will print a separate word list and an answer key if you choose those options.

When we began to use these programs with Marc we did so in a new setting. Part of his problem had been that teachers, despite their good intentions, had (in Marc's eyes) left him open to ridicule and embarrassment. We established a one-on-one environment with the microcomputer, with no human intervention, by assigning a computer for his study hall time and allowed a free-wheeling forty-five minutes with the machine.

The first time Marc sat down to the microcomputer, we knew we were on the right track. He worked with this very patient and tireless machine. It provided him with immediate feedback and positive reinforcement, not embarrassment. When he gave an incorrect answer, he simply tried again. His comment to me after school that first day was, "Mom, I can learn with the computer!"

Marc used the computer tutor at school and at home. As new words were added to the vocabulary programs, he spent much of his free time in front of the terminal nodding his head in acknowledgment of understanding. He would turn around and say, "Wow, Mom, I understand."

As his ability to understand the language of the mainstream text increased and sophistication with the microcomputer developed, it became necessary to offer more challenging material on disk. I began creating lessons with a major authoring system.

Major Authoring Systems

There are many authoring systems and languages that make writing interactive courseware possible. It is just that some are easier to use than others. Of the many that I have tried, my favorite is PILOT.

PILOT is a computer language created by John Starkweather, a physician at the University of California. It was designed as a tool for teachers who wanted to develop courseware that could be interactive through dialogue as well as drill-and-practice routines. Instead of being limited to the traditional true/false, multiple choice kinds of questions available with drill-and-practice authoring systems, PILOT allows narrative descriptions. It is possible to present a concept or describe something and then ask questions about the subject to determine if the student understands the material, all in the same lesson.

Today, a PILOT version is available for virtually every popular computer brand, but even within the same language, on the same brand, some editions are easier to use than others.

I used a program called EZ-PILOT for the Apple. I liked it because it was easy to use, yet allowed me to do a lot, even with only one disk drive.

EZ-PILOT works with eight core commands. With those eight the author can do just about anything including graphics, sound, even entering his own BASIC routines into the programs (if a programmer at heart). The power, however, comes from the ability to write concept material, ask a question, allow for a response, then match that response to any number of possible correct answers. If the response matches one of the correct answers, a reinforcement statement you have written will appear. If the response is incorrect, statements you have written, telling the user he was wrong, will appear but those statements can include why he was wrong. With this language, you can write courseware so interactive and so complete as to rival the most sophisticated courseware, and to do so without any programming skills. It will take a few hours to learn the commands, but once those are familiar, you are limited only by your imagination.

The success we had using EZ-PILOT allowed real progress closing the language gap and moving Marc into a second stage of microcomputer usage. Instead of just standard tutorial materials, we incorporated other software, including a typing tutor and word processing program.

The individual education plan that developed not only met his needs for academic success but became a far reaching plan to prepare him for real life. We wanted to give him programs that would meet every child's normal needs, not just the special needs imposed by his deafness. Typing tutors taught him to use the microcomputer, word processing became a tool for written language, and communications software gave him telephone use, etc. His deafness dictated the specific software choice, just as blindness would dictate other software to be used. The software exists to fill these "normal" needs, regardless of the handicap. What is important is to use that software as early as possible. A microcomputer and appropriate software give the handicapped individual the tools to live a far more normal life. By exposing handicapped children early, we can eliminate a portion of the handicap and replace it with growth—growth and learning that will affect the quality of life from that moment on.

Self-Expression

One of the most valuable uses of the microcomputer is the application of this tool for self-expression and the development of problem solving skills. This particular area of education for the handicapped is often neglected because other things appear to be more important. The need to learn facts, develop language, learn to read and write are solid and very important goals of education. But for many handicapped children, traditional methods of acquiring these skills simply do not work. For years the struggle to pass on these common elements of knowledge, by traditional methods, has gone on with varying degrees of success, depending on the severity of the handicap.

Much research has been done to discover and address the special problems of specific handicaps. However, much more needs to be done on how technology may improve the delivery of the known and still undiscovered solutions.

One project that did much to achieve a link between the technology of today and handicapped children was the Logo Group at the Artificial Intelligence Laboratory of the Massachusetts Institute of Technology. In his book, *Special Technology for Special Children*, E. Paul Goldenberg gives an account of his findings as a member of that group. But more importantly, he presents a well researched dialogue concerning what is known about learning disabilities associated with each handicap and ways the computer can be used to overcome the problems.

Goldenberg's account centers around the Logo language and the concepts built into Logo to foster discovery learning. His book outlines an alternative to the "right or wrong," "black or white" discipline used in special education. It centers on the development of skills to acquire learning, not on what to learn.

Microcomputers are ideally suited to the development of problem solving skills. Allowing a child to write programs, making the computer do what he or she wants it to, and developing the software for the task are problem solving at its best. To write a program is one thing; to have the program do what you expected the first time you attempt to run it is quite another. The span between the first writing and the first correct running is problem solving known as "finding the bugs." The number of bugs will be directly proportional to the logic, sequencing, and rational thinking that went into the first writing. The learning comes from the rewrite. The computer, the unforgiving machine, designed to operate under the digital commands of properly sequenced material and rejecting anything else, is a strong but fair taskmaster, and a powerful tool to teach problem solving skills.

Teaching programming to children used to be a problem, because of the languages used. Even "user friendly" languages such as BASIC were too complicated and foreign for many students, even those without learning disabilities. One answer is Logo, the language of children so eloquently depicted in Goldenberg's book. Chapter IV of this book deals with Logo and the role it can play in developing the skills necessary for learning.

Microcomputers are a new medium of learning. It would be tragic if the uses of these machines were to be relegated exclusively to reenactment of the older mediums in a new box instead of really using the tool to the fullest. As with any new medium, the period of investigation to prove its worth must take place. With the microcomputer, this has already happened. Business, industry, even agriculture have moved to incorporate the advantages of the microcomputer. They are embracing the change as a method to remove burdensome tasks, improve the quality of life of the masses, and reduce the cost of goods and services.

As the educational system tries to implement this tool there is the danger of trying to fit old ways into the new technology rather than letting the new tools lead the way to the intended goal. An example is the teacher who sees little problem with the microcomputer in math classes but supports a local movement to ban typing tutors from the school. Perhaps her best friend is the typing teacher and she wants to protect her job. More likely she lacks the ability to see that her friend's job is only part of the issue. Her friend has several options, including changing the typing curriculum to include the new technology. If she

Hints For Implementation

and her friend are unable to accept the change and are willing to deprive their students of an easier, more efficient way to learn just to protect the "old ways," they may have choosen the wrong profession. If the goal of education is to impart knowledge, then the tools used should be judged on how well they meet that goal.

Looking at the microcomputer as a tool for special education, it is possible to see many of the traditional educational goals achieved with the the help of this tool. Motivation, drill and practice, concepts, and the individual educational needs of each child can be effectively delivered through the microcomputer. Implementing the computer beyond those obvious applications, however, is the challenge.

Implementing real-life applications such as instant access to information, communications, and environmental control should become a part of the educational process. The use of peripherals such as modems, printers, speech synthesizers, light pens, and voice input devices is crucial to the development of skills that will be needed for microcomputer uses of the future. The peripherals are extensions of the microcomputer and in many cases are the key to bringing the ideal modification of environment to the handicapped. These peripherals also are the common interfaces to uses of the microcomputer as an everyday device.

Common uses of the modem as the interface of communications should become part of the educational experience. As the tool for deaf telephone use, the modem has opened a closed door. As the universal tool for information access and communications, it offers a host of learning experiences. It allows immediate access to information of choice, electronic encyclopedias, wire services, bulletin boards, electronic mail, banking and shopping. The microcomputer and modem offer real-life experience today and a peek at the future. Because the handicapped will become familiar with the computer and modem for their special needs, they will actually gain an advantage over their "normal" contemporaries in this vital area.

The microcomputer as a *learning* tool is not the same thing as the microcomputer as a *teaching* tool. I would like to share with you the story of Matt, a nine-year-old deaf child and his first experience with the microcomputer.

Matt was unable to use the telephone so his parents bought a modem to make their microcomputer into a communications tool. On the day of delivery, his mother called me to try out the system to be sure it was working properly. As we sat miles apart chatting back and forth, with our words appearing on the screen, Matt, I'm told, watched from a safe distance, unsure of how the computer was going to allow him to use the telephone and somewhat baffled at the stream of conversation taking place on the screen. I suggested that our nine-year-old son, Joey, could talk to Matt and perhaps make him a little less apprehensive about trying it. It was to be Joey's first time using the computer as a telecommunications device as well. After a few instructions on what to do, we let the kids take over.

First Joey: "Hi Matt, what are you doing." There was a delay, then ever so slowly the letters of reply began "hijoey" corrected to read, "Hijoey" and corrected again until "Hi, Joey."

Matt suddenly had a need for written language. Capital letters, commas, upper and lower case letters took on a new meaning that had not existed before. He was using communications, directed to him, as a model for his own language. He began to correct errors on his own because now there was a personal reason and a model to accomplish the task.

The boys have become good friends over the telephone. Joey calls Matt to chat about the latest video game or whatever nine year olds talk about. The important thing is that Matt loves the chance to use the microcomputer and modem as a means of communication and, by doing so, is improving his written language skills in a way never before possible. His mother said, "We had been trying to teach Matt rules for written language but we sure weren't getting very far. Now, he is learning by doing."

By using the computer as a learning tool, the knowledge gained is spiced with logic and reason. The child has a motive to retain the experience because it has personal meaning. Learning by doing is by no means a new concept; it is just that the microcomputer offers so many opportunities for this kind of experience. The discovery of a microcomputer and modem as a device to stimulate the growth of written language is but one such use. To use the potential of the microcomputer in more such learning situations is part of the challenge facing educators and parents alike.

A plan for implementation of the microcomputer in special education should include *all* elements of use—motivational uses, standard drill and practice, and most of all, as a stimulus for learning rather than just a teaching tool. The microcomputer offers a chance, never before available, to give equal opportunity or actual advantage to the handicapped. With its use, barriers to normal function fall and the chance for competition in "normal" society emerges.

Specific Disabilities
III

Ten percent of the world's population is handicapped, according to researchers from Johns Hopkins University. This startling statistic was presented at the *Johns Hopkins First National Search for Applications of Personal Computing to Aid the Handicapped.*

This year-long search effort, led by The Johns Hopkins University Applied Physics Laboratory, coincided with the United Nations International Year for Disabled Persons. Over nine hundred software developers submitted entries. The twenty-eight winning entries were displayed at the National Academy of Sciences in Washington, DC, in the fall of 1981.

The entries covered microcomputer applications for the blind, hearing impaired, deaf blind, movement handicapped, learning disabled, nonvocal and physically handicapped. Their collection represented the first nationwide attempt to find software and hardware applications for the handicapped.

The *Search* brought national attention to the potential of the microcomputer as a device to help handicapped individuals. Before the *Search*, countless individuals labored in obscurity, solving a particular problem for individuals or small groups by writing software and creating modified devices to meet their needs. But that is where it seemed to stop. There was no organized effort to disseminate the information nor any way to make the software available to the general population.

After the *Search*, a small but steady effort emerged to transmit general information about the microcomputer as a tool for the handicapped. In a few cases software shown in Washington was made available to consumers. The most dramatic effect, however, was the attention drawn to the overall need for software and the response from programming engineers and computer industry specialists. The problem of "technology for the handicapped" was being addressed by a pool of professional programmers, larger than a few dedicated people with a personal need, and the information barrier began to fall.

Although "need" was beginning to be recognized, that does not mean implementation was or is taking place. That barrier still exists, for reasons so elementary, so basic, as to go unrecognized or even acknowledged—*fear* of the microcomputer and lack of adequate information to overcome that fear. Many professionals who work with handicapped individuals are in a position to implement microcomputer technology for the handicapped. Most are not doing so, either because they do not know it exists (and I find that very hard to believe) or because they feel that they are not capable of gaining the necessary knowledge. They choose instead to ignore the entire subject.

Others who have taken the plunge into computer technology often do so with blinders on: They see only a small part of the overall picture. As Dr. Dolores Shanahan said in her paper, "The Computer—A Technology that Breaks the Sound Barrier," (*American Annals of the Deaf*, Volume 127, Number 5, 1982):

> *The question seems to be, "What is the primary role of the computer?"*
>
> *It seems to the author that educators are very much indeed like the blind man in the "Hindoo Fable" by John Godfrey Saxe. Six blind men went to see the elephant in the hope of learning about him. After feeling a different part of the elephant, each concluded that the animal was like a "wall, a spear, a snake, a tree, a fan, and a rope." All the observations were "partly in the right and all were in the wrong!"*

Only through understanding all uses of the microcomputer can we go beyond the fable's six blind men. A lack of understanding of various microcomputer uses can lead to less than full implementation and that is almost as serious as no implementation. Educational professionals must meet the challenge of their own misgivings. They must learn to recognize how valuable microcomputer technology can be and they must learn that they can take advantage of this tool even if they have no programming knowledge.

The development of software and hardware for handicapped users has increased since the Johns Hopkins *Search*. Each and every day, new products and modifications are being created. A new and wonderous road to equality for the handicapped is emerging. How and when handicapped children can take advantage of this new technology rests largely with the educational system. One can hope it will be soon.

Learning Disabled

The term *learning disabled* is a catch-all used to describe a large variety of handicaps. Research shows that somewhere between ten and twenty percent of school age children have specific learning disabilities—perceptual handicaps, minimal brain dysfunction, dyslexia, etc.

The U.S. government has one definition of the term *learning disabled*; there also are clinical, medical and practical definitions, and all seem to differ widely. For the purposes of this book the current government definition will be used. This definition is that learning disabled children are those children with normal IQs, who have difficulty in one or more of the following areas: oral expression, listening comprehension, written expression, basic reading skills, reading comprehension, math calculation or math reasoning skills. These children are found in mainstream education with support from special education professionals in the specific disability area.

The underlying causes of these conditions are so critical to effective service that I sometimes wonder why the system has chosen to bury their names as though they were dirty words. Personally, I am offended when someone waltzes around the condition of "deafness" with gloss-over terms like "hearing impaired" or "hearing difficulty." In most instances, the use of such terms has caused unnecessary confusion. The people with whom my son interacts, his teachers, all of them, need to know that he is deaf. I cannot tell you the hours that have been spent with mainstream teachers trying to undo their impressions of the label "hearing impaired" when a little honest, straightforward use of the term "deaf" would have served to identify the problem much more adequately, especially for Marc, for he is the one whose development depends on teachers who accurately understand his condition.

In keeping with the current homogeneous attitudes toward specific disabilities, there are some commonalities among the learning difficulties experienced by learning disabled children. One of these is the need for repetition of material. If current teaching methods are correct, repetition . . . repetition . . . repetition is a critical factor in overcoming certain disabilities. The process is tedious and time consuming. It is also one ideally suited to the microcomputer.

DRILL AND PRACTICE

Drill and practice, as a means of transmitting and retaining information, is perhaps the most common use of the microcomputer in education. The microcomputer and appropriate drill-and-practice software can provide a superior method of delivering certain academic skills. However, as is the case with most good things, there is the danger of overuse or, to be more precise, the *only* use of the microcomputer.

Advantages

First the good side: What is drill and practice on the microcomputer? In its most elementary form, it is question and answer formats (subject irrelevant) written by teachers, parents or programmers and presented to students on the microcomputer. The computer presents a question and the student answers. If the answer is correct, predetermined positive reinforcement is given. If the answer is incorrect, the program responds with "No, try again," or some other predetermined statement indicating incorrect response. In some programs the microcomputer counts the number of correct and incorrect responses making scoring available to the student and teacher. When this feature is present it is called a *management system.*

As a tool for teaching learning disabled students, drill and practice using the microcomputer has some very positive possibilities. Math facts, spelling, new vocabulary, any skill that requires repetitive presentation for comprehension is conducive to microcomputer use. Certainly these repetitive routines can be presented with paper and pencil, worksheets or flash cards. However, these traditional methods have drawbacks when compared to microcomputer presentation. The most critical of these is the problem of instilling motivation.

Immediate feedback is the strongest advantage that the microcomputer has over traditional teaching methods. When given the choice between worksheet drills and microcomputer drills, students universally opt for the microcomputer. When asked why, answers range from "It's more fun," to "It tells me when I goof."

"Fun" and "goof" are key words. How many students do you know would willingly do the same worksheet over and over again to learn a set of facts? Even if the teacher could immediately correct and hand back the worksheet (to make even the concept possible), the chances are pretty slim. Yet with microcomputer drill and practice it is not uncommon to see a child do the same math drill or spelling lesson over and over again, just because it's fun. Instead of "wrong" answers the child learns to think of incorrect responses as "goofs." This nonjudgmental attitude encourages repetition. If repetition is going to get the concept to the child, the microcomputer will sit there as long as the child is willing, and do it over and over again.

The immediate feedback capability of the microcomputer has advantages that can only be duplicated with an actual one-on-one human encounter. The act of writing down answers and waiting minutes, hours, even days for the paper to be corrected is the old, established way of doing things. When the correct answer arrives, the child must establish the concentration necessary to digest it and to make it relevant again, provided the paper is even reviewed. This is one of the many problems with the "testing" and "right/wrong" rituals of education, especially with learning disabled children. The microcomputer solves part of this problem. When working on a microcomputer that child is going to know when he is wrong *right now*, not days from now. He or she will get immediate correction and a chance for retention of the correct information. This sort of immediate feedback has been available with human interaction but not with paper and pencil drill.

With a microcomputer, the child is in charge of presentation and can exercise options at his discretion. Certainly there are far more sophisticated uses of the microcomputer available to foster this "learning by doing" concept, but even this most elementary drill-and-practice puts the child in control of his environment, which is a very important element when compared to the constant "teaching" that accompanies so much of the needed repetition in special education.

It would be nice if all our interaction with children could be done on our "good days," days when the world is right and so are we. Unfortunately, at least in my case, there are bad days, and the first ones to recognize the difference between the two are my children. It would be unrealistic to assume that all interactions between teacher and student are positive, pleasant encounters, just as unrealistic as it is to imagine parent and child without conflict. Human beings have emotions and sometimes they flare at inopportune times. No, I don't beat my children, but I'm sure I have been guilty of unfair emotional outbursts, using them as convenient targets of anger and frustration. This also happens in the classroom. It can't help but happen, especially when teachers and students are faced with the tedium that accompanies the mountains of drill and practice necessary with learning disabled children. By definition these children have disabilities they can do nothing about. Of all the children in the world who don't need a guilt trip over something they can't control, it's them.

The microcomputer, on the other hand, doesn't yell, doesn't have bad days, or make a fool of itself with emotional outbursts. When people say that the microcomputer is an "unemotional tutor," believe it. The use of a microcomputer for drill and practice will remove a very tiresome role for the teacher or parent and the replacement can be counted on to fill the need efficiently, unemotionally, and tirelessly.

Yet another attribute of drill and practice via microcomputer is the tutorial package that can be transported with the student to the home environment. Since we are talking about interactive materials that can function without another human being in the equation, we can extend the opportunity for reinforcement with less effort by fewer people. I was taught, and firmly believe, that a handicapped child will not succeed without reinforcement at home. I also know that dirty laundry, three other children, a husband and job can severely limit the amount of time available for reinforcement. I am not suggesting that the microcomputer can replace mom, but it can help her out when the baby is crying or dinner must be fixed.

Disadvantages

So much for praise. There also is a not-so-good side of drill and practice by microcomputer for learning disabled children.

There are some dangers inherent in using the microcomputer for drill and practice even though none of them have anything to do with the microcomputer itself. The dangers are:

1. Drill and practice will become the only use; and

2. Little care will be given to the software selection.

Microcomputer programs must meet the needs of the child, just as any other drill-and-practice routine. Software is not appropriate just because it is presented electronically, but it should also meet some academic skill goal. Just as with any other teaching medium, the language must be appropriate, positive and negative feedback must be given and any necessary hints or opportunities for additional practice must be provided.

The best software is designed for user control—what is on the screen can be read and comprehended, and the user decides when to proceed. Some software uses a timing sequence that forces the user forward when the software says, even if the student isn't ready. That kind of software is particularly inappropriate for learning disabled students.

The best drill-and-practice software will often be packaged on disks or tapes that can be customized for the individual needs of the child through authoring systems. Here, exactly what you want to present to the child will be entered and available to the student. This type of software can be prepared by the teacher, aide or parent with no more time or effort than preparation of a worksheet, perhaps less. Drill-and-practice (mini) authoring systems are available for all popular microcomputer brands and learning to use them is a very simple procedure.

Don't expect the student to sit in front of the terminal all day and do drill and practice even if he wants to (and many do). Change software, even the authoring system contents. Boredom is still boredom, even at the microcomputer. If the skill goal is going to take weeks to acquire, vary the software accordingly.

Drill and practice, by microcomputer and appropriate software, is by a long margin the most popular use of the microcomputer in education because it is easy to do and nonthreatening to the educators themselves. Most of those who feel threatened by technology can come to terms with drill and practice without changing the way they teach. This "condition of the mind," this "keep the microcomputer in its place" attitude is by far the greatest danger in using drill and practice. In order for the microcomputer actually to be a benefit and not just another way to practice $4 \times 4 = 16$, teachers are going to have to change the way they teach the handicapped. There is nothing wrong with using the microcomputer to teach $4 \times 4 = 16$, but there is something drastically wrong if that is *all* the microcomputer is allowed to do.

AUDIO AND VISUAL—ADDED PORTS OF ENTRY

Many learning disabled children, for whatever medical reason, have difficulty using reading by itself to acquire information. Here the microcomputer can be extremely helpful in a variety of configurations.

Synchronizing a tape recorder with the text on the screen of a microcomputer can be accomplished with the addition of a special switch. One such product is the CCD (Cassette Control Device) from Hartley Courseware. Designed for the Apple II and IIe, this inexpensive controller presents students with a wide variety of drill and practice, authoring systems and concept materials with simultaneous audio and visual presentation. The teacher or parent prepares a tape recording according to directions that accompany the software. The microcomputer, software, tape recorder and CCD then combine to present the student with both visual and audio stimulation.

Another method of achieving visual and audio presentation is through speech synthesis. A system that seems to work very well is the Echo II speech board for the Apple II or IIe. This synthesizer can "speak" any text file (software without graphics) simultaneously with the screen presentation. This breakthrough of reasonably priced speech synthesis (the board costs about $150.00) will have a dramatic effect on the population who can benefit from or who require dual ports of entry to receive information.

The drill-and-practice or computer assisted instruction uses of the microcomputer that have been covered here are enhancements of existing methods of teaching the learning disabled. They may well be more motivating, easier, more cost-effective methods of delivery but they are still just enhancements. They put "old methods into the new electronic box," much the same way that the pioneers of the 1940s and early 1950s first used television. Remember those days, when television sent pictures of the radio studio to the viewers? The performers did nothing with the visual capability of the new medium because they did not understand it or know how to use it. It took many years before the real power of the medium was even explored.

The same is true with the current educational uses of the microcomputer. The comfortable, tried and true methods will not change easily. People are inherently comfortable with the old and apprehensive of the new. The tragedy is that in many instances change is not the issue. Much of what has been proven educationally sound will not change but rather be made better, easier, and more complete. There are, however, teaching and learning possibilities unique to the microcomputer that will require some change in attitudes.

Removing the Pencil and Paper Blockade

Most learning disabled children have difficulty with pencil and paper tasks. The reasons may differ, but generally, if a request for written expression is made, there are poor results, especially when the handicap is compounded by the request for creative thinking. An example is written language. A child, given the task of writing a sentence or paragraph, must first overcome the crude instrument that, when committed to paper, can only be removed by creating a messy eraser smudge ... stop ... erase ... try again. The child must overcome the original handicap plus one imposed upon him, then apply concentration sufficient to be creative. That's an awful lot to ask from someone already having problems, especially when the appearance of the results will reflect the struggle, not the accomplishment. All that effort and a messy, dirty paper to show the teacher.

The alternative provided by a microcomputer and word processing programs for learning disabled children is equal to the reinvention of written language, designed specifically for their needs. Strong words? Yes, but strong medicine needs strong words. If nothing else, maybe someone will try to disprove the statement and, in the process, actually begin using the tool and discover its worth. I guarantee they can't disprove the statement and at this point, I'm willing to try just about anything to gain wider understanding and implementation of word processing for learning disabled children.

Word processing software provides the ability to commit written language to paper electronically. It is a word handling device. The words, sentences, paragraphs, punctuation, etc., are put into the microcomputer and displayed on the screen as they are being written. When the work is complete, the end result can be reproduced on paper via a printer connected to the computer.

Written language skills, for the language handicapped, are some of the most difficult objectives to achieve. There is the tedious effort that goes into the organization of thoughts, the laborious task of writing them down, searching for the right words or expression only to desire change. Change, with paper and pencil or typewriter, means recopying, again and again. These stumbling blocks of change, reworking and recopying are enough to discourage anyone. For the language handicapped, they present an almost insurmountable barrier that crushes the mental process of composition and expression.

With a word processing program, many of these arduous tasks are eliminated. The word processor allows changes in the written text with simple keyboard commands. Letters and words can be changed or erased altogether. One can rearrange paragraphs, correct spelling (or have the computer do it automatically), insert new words or phrases, change punctuation, insert and replace at will. Rewrite means changing or deleting only the affected words or lines. There is no need to retype or recopy the entire paper. Once complete, the document can be printed and the paper handed in as a neat, readable assignment that represents the expressive capability of the student.

As a teaching tool, word processing software is an enormous asset. The teacher or parent can correct the document. The student need only return to the microcomputer, pull up the story from disk or cassette storage, and with keyboard commands, correct the assignment to the edited standards and again send the document to the printer to generate a letter-perfect paper—a source of pride and accomplishment.

Not only does the word processing program improve the possibility of expressive written language but it gives the child a source of pride, when the effort is complete. That pride can move the child to even greater effort and becomes a motivator to overcome the disability.

The population that would benefit most from this communication aid is the language handicapped, yet in the recent *Symposium on Research and Utilization of Educational Media for Teaching the Deaf— Microcomputers in Education of the Hearing Impaired* (American Annals of the Deaf, September, 1982) only passing mention is made of word processing as a language development tool. The 1983 ACLD (Association for Children with Learning Disabilities) International Conference held in Washington, DC, included nearly two hundred presentations, yet only twelve involve instruction, and there was *no* mention of word processing as a tool for the education of learning disabled children.

Typing skills are critical for effective use of word processing as a tool for the development of written language. Microcomputer typing tutors should be introduced for the learning disabled as early as fingers can span the keyboard. These skills are crucial to efficient use of the microcomputer. There is little question as to the need for typing skills; however, actually introducing them as part of elementary grade curriculum has received little support.

Microcomputer based typing tutors and word processing can represent the road to successful written language where pencil and paper have failed. As E. Paul Goldenberg stated in his book, *Special Technology for Special Children*, "Throughout this book, I refer to deaf children, cerebral palsied children, and autistic children, sometimes almost in the same breath. I have no intention of suggesting that these children's life problems are all the same, nor do I believe that the solutions are all the same. However, it is not their 'special' needs with which I am primarily concerned, but their 'normal' needs. What binds these children together also binds them to the rest of humanity; their needs to have an enjoyable and estimable life and to be able to interact satisfyingly with their environment and its people, things, and demands. Sometimes we require special techniques and technology to help us meet our needs. Only when these are wanting are we truly handicapped."

The "techniques and technology" to help learning disabled children develop new and useful communication skills exist. The only question remaining is when they will become a reality within the educational system.

The typing tutor/word processing uses of the microcomputer will require a change in attitudes among teaching professionals. These applications are unique to this machine. Learning to use them as teaching devices is relatively simple, but it is a change. All of the educationally sound procedures for teaching language handicapped children remain. No retraining or change of teaching strategies is required, just the inclusion of a new tool for the delivery system. The microcomputer and typing tutor are no more difficult to use than a movie projector. Word processing programs may require a little more time to learn, but learning what commands do which tasks, etc., is an uncomplicated routine easy to master in a day or two.

Removing the pencil and paper blockade for learning disabled children is nothing more than allowing the use of today's technology. A microcomputer and printer along with typing tutor software and a word processing program does the trick. It sounds so easy because it *is* easy and useful, beyond any other set of tools.

Yet to be discussed are the discovery learning applications of the microcomputer for the learning disabled child. These may well represent the most important microcomputer application of all. Logo, the discovery learning computer language for children, is the subject of Chapter V. There are discovery learning applications of Logo for all children and I will save the discussion of this language until we look at microcomputer uses in other disability areas.

Deaf and Hearing Impaired

Hearing impaired children can use the microcomputer in much the same way as learning disabled children. All of the drill-and-practice, typing tutor, word processing uses apply just as readily here. There are, however some specialized uses that are designed especially for the deaf.

Children who were deaf at birth or became deaf before they learned how to speak live in an isolated world that prevents them from acquiring communication skills naturally. They cannot hear others speak, and therefore are unable to acquire intelligible speech patterns. Without intervention, these children will never be able to process information presented in standard English or to gain any ability to communicate interactively with the hearing world. Traditional methods of intervention used in education, both oral and sign, can improve the situation. However, those dealing with educating the deaf may soon have available a technology capable of enhancement equal of those dreamed of by Alexander Graham Bell. Mr. Bell's chief contribution to communication, of course, was the telephone. His invention was conceived from his desire to aid the deaf, and in the process, he created the single most important device for mass communication in the history of man. It is ironic that the telephone was useless for the very people he was trying to help, the deaf. Now, with the emergence of the microcomputer and modem, Bell's dream of long-distance communications capability for the deaf is becoming a reality. Before discussion of the one-hundred-year dream, however, it is necessary to look at a one-hundred-year war.

The controversies that surround deaf education rage with little purpose, except love of battle by the combatants. Oral communication purists versus total communication theorists have fought their battle for at least one hundred years. There are those who want the world to learn ASL (American Sign Language) in the hopes that a wider communication base will develop for those individuals without oral skills. On the other side there is the group who consider it "the end of the world" if a child is exposed to sign language. Unfortunately, the battle has tended to sap everyone's energy and divert attention from the microcomputer and the language development tool it represents. The micro is all but being ignored, except as a drill-and-practice device.

The battle that continues over sign versus oral communication for deaf children is the most outrageous disservice to the actual needs of these children that has ever clouded professional judgment. While the two contingents argue over who is right, deaf children are born and ill-equipped parents must make communication and education decisions on behalf of their children. These parents (and I am one) are confronted with decisions that will have life-long consequences for their children, yet the parents usually do not have the knowledge necessary to make a reasonable decision. They must choose the form of communications and education their child will receive while the professionals stand back waiting for the opportunity to say "I told you so." The professionals offer little to the parents facing the decision making process, but they are more than willing to take credit for the successes that occur and use the failures (deaf children unable to communicate) to fuel the fires of their raging battle.

There is no way this book or any other single effort is going to solve the one-hundred-year war or, for that matter, give credence to either side. The questions that separate the two sides defy logic and rational thinking, and any attempt to interject some would serve only to confuse both sides. My efforts will center on keeping the microcomputer out of the war zone and fostering its use to help all deaf and hearing impaired children.

Applications of the microcomputer for the deaf include lip reading training software as well as sign language and finger spelling programs. The visual presentation capability of the microcomputer allows hearing persons as well as hearing impaired to use drill-and-practice routines. Anyone who wants to learn finger spelling, for instance, can do so with a computer tutor. This innovative use of the microcomputer can allow families and friends of deaf individuals to learn sign communications just as quickly and effectively as the hearing impaired individuals themselves.

Learning to communicate is the primary challenge of the deaf. For the child without hearing, there is no auditory stimulation, therefore no natural verbal language development. Everything this child will learn about language must come from imposed or artificial means.

Applification, through the use of hearing aids, lip reading and articulation training are the tools commonly available for development of speech for the deaf child. These tools require enormous amounts of concentration, endless listening for clues (a very tiring experience) and constant repetition with no auditory feedback, just encouragement from parents or teachers. The student has no way of knowing how close he or she is to the correct pronunciation of a word or phrase except the honesty of the person attempting to teach.

A microcomputer, software, and a voice entry system can easily be combined to produce a vocalization training device. One such system was developed and entered in the Johns Hopkins *Search*. Although the components (TRS-80 Model I and Vox Box with a total cost of $600) are no longer manufactured, efforts to convert the system to Model III and other voice entry methods are under way. Similar systems that use the Apple II are being developed.

As long ago as 1945, Bell Laboratories developed a visible speech translator that produced visual pictures of speech patterns for articulation training. However, it was too expensive for general use. Now with microcomputer technology, a low-cost version of the Bell Labs device is almost a reality.

The Johns Hopkins software search revealed many applications for the deaf using the microcomputer. First prize ($10,000) went to Harry Levitt, a speech and hearing professor at the City University of New York, for his portable telephone communication system. He combined an inexpensive TRS-80 pocket computer and a miniature TRS-80 telephone interface to provide access to public telephones. This and other telephone uses for the deaf are bringing us closer to Alexander Graham Bell's dream.

The deaf and hearing impaired have long been isolated from any method of distant communication, short of written words in letter form and transmitted by the mail. Not only is this cumbersome and slow, but in an emergency it is totally useless. In the early 1960s Western Union donated a batch of outdated teletype machines to the deaf community for the purpose of communications over existing telephone lines. A creative young engineer, Bob Weitbrecht, developed a modem (*m*odulator-*dem*odulator) to convert key strokes to Baudot codes (audible tone signals) that could be transmitted over telephone lines. This allowed the Rube Goldberg-type teletypes to become the first useable communications system for the deaf. The Telecommunication Teletypewriters for the Deaf (TTYs as they are called) and their owners became a small network of users. However, the disbursement of these machines was slow, spotty geographically and use never did become widespread.

The limited use of TTYs is traceable to several factors. First, the machines and the Baudot language of transmission are used only by the deaf community and a few service organizations with a need or desire to communicate with the deaf. TTYs are not compatible with the American Standard for Communications Information Interchange (ASCII) code used by microcomputers. This limits their effective communications to other deaf persons, and blocks communication with the hearing world. Second, TTYs are dedicated communication devices with no other use. Making specialized devices is expensive, and the cost was prohibitive for many deaf persons. Third, effective use of the machines requires typing skills and typing has not been taught as a communications skill for the deaf, but just as a business skill for a very select few.

As technology developed, the old teletypes were replaced by modern style electronic TDDs (Telecommunication Devices for the Deaf). However, these machines duplicated the shortcomings of the TTYs with dedicated communication uses and Baudot-only transmission code capabilities. In 1982, the entire TTY-TDD network was estimated to consist of between 25,000 and 60,000 machines, depending on the source of the count. Either figure is woefully inadequate to serve a total deaf population of 1.7 million and a hearing impaired population of 13 million in the United States alone.

In July of 1982 a major breakthrough occured when AT&T (American Telephone and Telegraph) granted a request to certify microcomputers as TDDs. This request, submitted by my husband, Budd Hagen, asked AT&T for the same toll rate reductions for microcomputers that traditional TDDs received. Joseph Heil, AT&T's director for handicapped services, granted that request and directed all Bell operating companies to honor such requests in the future. These toll rate reductions cover all long-distance interstate calls placed by a hearing or speech handicapped individual who has requested the service.

Budd is the editor of our newspaper dealing with special education and handicap uses of the microcomputer. He submitted the AT&T request on behalf of our deaf, thirteen-year-old son, Marc. Budd's larger purpose, however, was to widen communication capability for all deaf and hearing impaired individuals. After receiving the national certification for interstate reductions, he requested the same accommodation from our local Bell operating company, to cover intrastate calls. Vern Haglund, director of Northwestern Bell's Telecommunication Center for Disabled Customers (TCDC) in Minneapolis, Minnesota granted the request and microcomputers were added to the list of equipment qualifying for the intrastate toll reductions as well.

Budd then went one step further. The Public Utilities Commission had recently directed Northwestern Bell to offer a low-cost loan to allow purchase of special equipment. The loans were to be offered to handicapped individuals covering a wide variety of equipment designed to aid disabled persons in use of the telephone. The original loan program did not cover microcomputers, but Budd, fresh from the victory covering the toll rate reductions, requested Northwestern Bell to include microcomputers in the loan program. To his great delight, the request was granted. This meant, of course, that speech or hearing handicapped individuals, in Minnesota, who have Northwestern Bell telephone sevice could purchase a microcomputer, modem and printer, (all or one) with low-interest financing by Northwestern Bell. More importantly, this meant that speech or hearing impaired children could get microcomputers at home for communication uses, and also gain access to an educational tool—a tool capable of removing many of the obstacles resulting from the handicap.

The worldwide communication capabilities of the microcomputer are discussed in Chapter V. However, the educational values of telecommunication will be touched on here.

For the deaf, telecommunication provides a use for written language, a use that gives the deaf motivation to learn. In all the years that I have watched my son struggle with written language there was never a meaningful reason for him to acquire the skills. There was also little opportunity. His educational environment seemed to focus on answers to questions, right or wrong, black or white, often rhetorical questions for thought stimulation, but little request for expression, especially written expression. The few opportunities there were for written language development were stifled by lack of experience and very poor tools (the pencil and paper) coupled with very little motivation. Having the feeling that you will fail miserably at the task because you don't know how to perform it and knowing this is another "test" of your nonexistent ability does little to spark desire. In my son's view, written language had become a rotten, miserable task and one he would go to any lengths to avoid.

Telecommunications via the microcomputer, on the other hand, not only gives opportunity for written language, it demands it. The system *is* written language, transmitted over telephone lines. If one is to communicate using a microcomputer, the words, the text, the conversation must be typed into the microcomputer. In the case of one-on-one personal conversations, the transmission occurs instantaneously as the letters are typed. It is possible to prepare materials in advance for transmission (text file) and send the entire file after it has been written and edited, but in either case, the actual act of writing the material must take place.

In practice, this reason for written language can dramatically improve the development of written language skills for the deaf and hearing impaired.

Again, I will use my son as an example. Quite honestly, I would prefer to use others, but there are few examples from which to draw. The use of telecommunication via microcomputer for the deaf is so new, I wasn't able to find any actual "in school" educational applications in progress.

Marc was introduced to telecommunications at home. Because he is deaf, he has never been able to use the telephone in its normal configuration. The addition of an Apple Cat II modem (made by Novation) to the Apple II microcomputer sitting in our living room was to be the first "tool" that would give him access to the phone.

We had considered adding a traditional TTY or TDD for telecommunications, but our observations of the limited and dedicated use seemed to make it a poor investment choice. We also saw it as a device that would perpetuate bad language examples, because use of these devices is primarily by other deaf individuals. In addition to the potential for limited written language models, there are a number of complex abbreviations and shortcuts that have developed within the TTY-TDD communications system. These, coupled with the written language skills of the users, have developed into a language that has very little in common with standard written English.

Because Marc wanted and needed use of the telephone, we saw the written language demands of telecommunications as a means to develop his written language skills. The opportunity to communicate with hearing people and other microcomputer users through bulletin boards and on-line systems presented good language models. His desire to use the telephone provided the motivation. Between the two, a solid learning experience developed that gave him both the experience and desire to improve his skills.

Marc's first personal contact happened to be with a sixteen-year-old hearing boy. Marc's first observation was how fast the boy could type. The words literally flew across the screen. Marc's first reaction was "WOW," followed immediately by. "I want to learn to type that fast," resulting in a self-imposed ritual of typing tutor practice to enhance his own typing ability.

Another observation was the language structure itself. Not "this is a noun" or "this is a verb," but rather a personal communication requirement to express thoughts clearly and the need for a consistent model to emulate. Marc has consistently shown an ability to attempt emulation of the language structure he sees on the screen in his conversational interaction with that language. Perhaps he is relearning English as his language, now that he has a consistent model to follow. Obviously, he has not had access to a flowing input of language. His auditory ability is very limited and since lip reading is only effective with about one quarter of spoken English, there is no way he could have a consistent flow of language structure from which to learn. It may be that through written language, with a purpose, natural acquisition forces are stimulated and used.

Regardless of *how* Marc is actually using his new avenue to written language development or what forces are at play, his written language skills are showing marked growth through use of personal telecommunication. At this time there is little research to offer any clues to the overall impact of this type of tool, but his obviously improved written language skills make it imperative that we continue to provide the opportunity and to encourage the educational system to incorporate the technology that would allow him to pursue this technique at school.

In the special education setting, the uses of telecommunications could include many interactive dialogue situations demanding written language with a personal purpose. Just a simple bulletin board concept, where interactive dialog could take place between teacher and student or microcomputer and student, or scanning for personal mail, messages left by other students or teachers and soliciting a response, or conversations, dialogue, even questions posed in written form could become a regular part of language development. As I sit here, I am trying to guess the number of times Marc may have been asked to pose a question in relation to the number of times he has been asked to answer one, especially in written form. Not many, I'm afraid. Somehow, it has become standard procedure to ask questions of children and expect responses. Answering questions, right/wrong, is the backbone of education. In special education, there seems to be little reciprocal opportunity for the child to ask the questions. Even more importantly, there is little training in the skill of asking questions in the first place. The desire to pull answers out of children seems to supercede any other consideration, even that of giving handicapped children the tools or ability to ask questions about their surroundings.

Suppose resource and research materials were accessible through microcomputer (as they currently are) and further suppose that students could use that material. Suppose the system were designed to answer questions instead of ask them. How long would it take for a child to learn to *ask* questions instead of simply responding to questions?

It certainly didn't take long for Marc to discover that by asking questions, he could get answers, especially if he phrased them correctly. He chose to ask his questions via telephone, a common enough procedure for the hearing world, but one formerly unavailable for the deaf. Once given the capability of telecommunications, Marc immediately discovered bulletin boards. By posing a question or asking for information about a subject on a bulletin board he could get responses from people outside of his family and get vastly different answers, which amazed him at first.

His first communication placed on a bulletin board read as follows:

> *My name is Marc Hagen. I'm 13 years old, and I would like to talk to other people my age and others. I am deaf and this is the only way I can use a telephone. Leave me your telephone number in my dad's mail box, (Budd Hagen) and I'll call you.*

New friends? Yes. A reason for written language? Yes. An actual tool for the development of written language for the deaf? I believe it is. What is probably more important is Marc's view of telecommunications. In Marc's own words, "I almost copy the words that other people use. . . . The way they use them helps me learn to correct my language. I call Shawn (a friend), and I can ask him a question about anything. It helps me like a teacher helps me. When I see how Shawn talks, I want to talk the same and I practice so I can talk the same way."

To Marc, using this typed communication capability is "talking." He is using the telephone and every reference to telephone use he has seen means talking over the telephone. I have not corrected this misuse of terms, because to me, the semantics are not important, the communication is.

DEVELOPING ORAL SKILLS WITH A WRITTEN LANGUAGE BASE

Marc seems to be developing oral skills on the same level and at about the same pace of improvement as his written language development. Noticeable differences in spoken vocabulary usage, syntax, verb tenses, etc., seem to be directly relevant to "learned" written language. Not all of the spoken vocabulary is used in his written language, yet there is definitely a spoken use pattern that reflects newly acquired written language use. It is too early to tell if this trend will continue or if there is any real connection between the two. However, the improvements in spoken language structure to date certainly indicate some connection between them. At this point there are enough encouraging signs to try to keep some examples of spontaneous written language and recordings of oral conversation for comparison with later samples. These may give some insight into how written language will affect the development of spoken language for prelingually deaf children, if at all. With just one such unscientific "observation" as the sole source of data, there is not very much to go on, but it may stimulate additional research into the subject.

Educational applications of the microcomputer for deaf and hearing impaired children entail the use of software and peripherals commonly available. There is nothing difficult or complicated about any of the uses. The microcomputer configuration best suited for use is one with a modem, for telecommunications, and preferably one that transmits in both ASCII and Baudot. This will allow the user to communicate with the traditional TDD network as well as the millions of microcomputer users. The addition of a printer is a necessity for all educational applications if word processing is going to be a part of the training. Then it is a matter of software choice, and the standard typing tutor, drill and practice, authoring systems, word processing and communications software become the basic list. Using the software and building an educational environment that utilizes these new tools to their fullest potential is not difficult.

Presenting deaf children with the technology of the information and communication age can remove a great deal of the isolation that has been so much a part of their lives. They can look forward to equality in exchange of information, something that was impossible just a few years ago. Telecommunications, the visual exchange of information, is the key. The tools that will allow deaf children to use telecommunications must be given to them—all the tools, the typing skills, the language, word processing, the hardware and software for access to the hearing world.

Blind and Visually Impaired

As we put the finishing touches on a newspaper article featuring applications of microcomputer technology for the blind and visually impaired, I remember being struck with one thought—never again will the blind be subject to someone else's choice of literature. The microcomputer of today could well replace readers, armies of volunteer Braillers, and instead allow blind individuals the freedom to choose their own written text, gain access to that information and do so without the intervention of a second person.

All of this potential and much more exists through uses of the microcomputer and common peripherals. A speech synthesizer can be made to speak any text file through software control. One very powerful software source for control of the synthesizers is the Braille-Edit program from Raised Dot Computing. This particular program (for the Apple II and IIe) will allow a speech synthesizer to speak the file and will allow for creation of new files (with a very useful text editor as part of the software) either through standard keyboard entry of text or through a Braille keyboard simulated on the Apple. In addition, the software also will convert those same text files to grade II Braille for output on several modified printers or to the VersaBraille for paperless Braille. The software can also convert Braille files from the Versa-Braille into standard text files for screen or printer output of standard text for sighted persons.

The mating of the VersaBraille to the Apple II microcomputer provides a very powerful word processing system for the Braille reading blind. The program allows a sighted person to enter text on the Apple, translate it into grade II, and transfer the material to the Versa-Braille. The program also allows reformatting of text in ways that are impossible on a VersaBraille.

The man behind the Braille-Edit software is David Holladay. Here is his description of the software and how it was developed:

Some of the most exciting products of the computer revolution are the paperless Braillers, talking terminals, and paper Braille printers that have enabled blind persons to obtain jobs in the burgeoning high technology fields formerly restricted to sighted persons. The thrust of my work is to increase the communication between blind and sighted persons, not just to make another computer terminal for the blind.

My wife is a blind mathematics professor at Bucknell University. Last year, with the financial help of the Wisconsin Division of Vocational Rehabilitation, she bought a VersaBraille paperless Brailler, which she used to write her Ph.D. thesis. However, once it was written in Braille, she was faced with the task of making a print copy. It was not an easy job to read a little bit at a time from the VersaBraille (in grade II and Nemeth code), and then type it out on an IBM Selectric. She had to keep track of three typeballs and the current carriage position (for superscripts or subscripts). I wish I had a nickel for each time I heard "David, what line am I on now?" As a computer programmer experimenting with an Apple II, I realized that this was a task for a computer.

Holladay tackled and solved the problem and many more when he wrote the Braille-Edit software. Here he describes some of the uses:

First I wrote a series of programs which I call Braille-Edit. These include a Braille-oriented text editor (a text editor used like an electronic Braillerwriter), a grade II translator, a reverse translator, and tranfer programs. Now I can take anything written on the Apple II, translate it to grade II, and then transfer it to the VersaBraille. Caryn can read it and make any changes she wants on the VersaBraille. Then I can transfer the copy back to the Apple, translate the grade II back to regular English and print it out. By giving two commands, the program will use a Braille character set on the CRT screen, and the Apple keyboard will act like a standard seven-key Braille keyboard (with no modification to the Apple!). This can also be useful to a sighted Braillist preparing material in a technical Braille code, such as mathematics or music.

Holladay's software provides a character-oriented text editor; the command refers to characters and numbers of characters rather than to lines. Commands are present to move the cursor, indicate where the next character will be placed, insert, delete, etc. On a VersaBraille such changes have to be individually indicated. According to Holladay, "The VersaBraille is a wonderful machine, but it is somewhat limited in its editing capabilities. Editing commands on a VersaBraille affect only one page (1,000 character limit) at a time."

One of the strongest features of the Braille-Edit software is its ability to support speech synthesizers. As a result, the same program on the same computer can easily be used by blind *and* sighted users. Using synthetic speech, the program can be used independently by a blind person without a VersaBraille. Users of the software tell the microcomputer how they want to use the program. A sighted user can use the Apple keyboard and the video screen. A blind user could ask the microcomputer to output via synthetic voice.

As a means of generating grade II Braille, Braille-Edit shines again. The software will support the RESUS, Thiel, the LED-120 and the Sagem. If a person has a bit of home-tinkering capability, it will also work with a modified Diablo daisywheel-type printer, the Cramner modified Perkins Brailler or an IBM Braille typewriter, driven with an ETF (Electric Typing Fingers) solenoid control.

The educational applications of software such as Braille-Edit are endless. The simple translation from Braille to English, English to Braille or to speech, of any written materials, opens doors long closed. I remember one teacher of the vision impaired who commented, "You mean I won't have to use my Braille Eraser any more . . ." as she tore a page of Braille text with an error near the bottom of the page into two pieces. Just the ability to create Braille materials prior to embossing will save this teacher many tedious hours of manual Brailling, and with the editing capability, produce errorless Braille besides.

Many uses of the microcomputer for the vision impaired require little more than the microcomputer and software that uses a larger character set. E-Z PILOT (for the Apple II), the authoring system referred to previously, carries the ability to generate large letters and numerals on the screen using Higher Text, from Synergistic Software. By using control commands that are part of E-Z PILOT, the text written by the teacher can be large capitals, double wide letters, or double sized letters. With another control command, a choice of ten different colors can be added. The lesson can be prepared using this large type capability and presented in this fashion as well.

The graphics and color capabilities of microcomputer presentation can add much to sight stimulation. Just as with any materials, however, bigger is not always better, and care must be used to present materials actually useable. High-resolution screens offer much cleaner lines and far more precise definitions of shapes and characters. Care in selection of both screen resolution and software is advised.

Perhaps the single most dramatic use of today's microcomputer technology for the blind and visually impaired is the voice or speech synthesis capabilities. From the educational side, many commercially available programs can be used directly with synthesizers. This means that blind students will be able to use the same programs as sighted students by having the synthesizers speak the text. There are technical reasons why all programs will not work with a synthesizer and those center around the DOS (Disk Operating System) commands. However, the Sensory Aids Foundation of Palo Alto, CA, and other groups are adapting a broad range of educational software for voice output. As software publishers become aware of the need for materials that can be used with a synthesizers, the problem of software that cannot be spoken should diminish.

Access to general print information, personal electronic mail and all the other features of telecommunications are available through the microcomputer with speech synthesis. This same information, once down-loaded to the microcomputer, can be embossed into grade II Braille by one of the Braille print configurations mentioned above. These options present a major breakthrough for the blind because they give access to information without requiring intervention by sighted helpers. These options can provide a free flow of data to and from the blind in their choice of output method, at the time they chose.

The interchange of written information between the blind and sighted persons now can be done with a choice of four separate output methods: screen, speech, printer, or grade II Braille printer. The conversion of this information is done by the microcomputer at will. This instantaneous conversion capability represents the essence of this technology for the blind and vision impaired. The educational and vocational opportunities are obvious, because the technology eliminates the major obstacle to the exchange of information.

The microcomputer offers Braille training programs as well. Raised Dot Computing (David Holladay again) offers software for the Apple II and IIe that teaches and drills sighted persons in grade II Braille. Rules and contractions are displayed on the television screen. At appropriate times, the user is presented with sample text to enter in Braille. The Apple keyboard acts like a Braillewriter and displays the entered Braille cells on the monitor. When the drill has been entered, the computer compares the entered Braille with the current versions, and shows any discrepancies in reverse video. Usually when Braille transcribers are trained, it takes a long time to correct drills, so this program shows real promise in improving transcriber training.

Offerings of software and peripherals to allow blind and vision impaired individuals to interact with microcomputers, both from an input and output mode, are growing. With the use of these aids, even programming the computer is possible. Large-size character sets for the visually impaired or speech output for the blind allows verification of programming input by these individuals, just as successfully as a sighted person can do with standard equipment. Just add the proper "tools" to the computer and it becomes just as powerful for the blind as it is for anyone else. This is pointed out in another excerpt from Holladay's abstract.

> *Many sighted math professors have commented on the quality of Caryn's math printouts (which are usually duplicated so they can be used as class handouts). They ask how they could use the program, and are disappointed to find out that they first have to learn the Braille math code. To rectify this imbalance and to correct the disadvantage that sighted math professors have in this area, I will probably write a math word processor program for sighted people. No user need know that at the heart of the system is a translator of the Braille math code.*

Mentally Retarded

A good friend told me I would be getting a telephone call from a mother of a five-year-old, nonvocal TMR (Trainable Mentally Retarded) little girl. The mother, I was told, was looking for help for her daughter through a microcomputer, and thought I might be able to give her some advice.

At the time, my experience with microcomputer applications for such a situation was limited to second- and third-hand reports of a few programs and research projects in progress, but little actual knowledge of software that might be applicable. We decided that sharing our experiences with our deaf son, and microcomputer technology in general, was all we could offer. However, in due course, the call was received and the visit set up, limitations not withstanding.

When the parents and five-year-old Kathy arrived, we chatted in the dining room. I asked several questions regarding Kathy: did she watch television, attention span, etc., and was told, "Yes, Kathy likes television." I asked our guests to wait for a few minutes.

At the time, our living room was the computer lab. Along one wall a typing-height table held three different brands of microcomputers. I had no idea how Kathy might react to the situation, so I shut down everything but the Texas Instrument 99/4A microcomputer. I chose TI because of the software I had available, an early reading series by Scott, Foresman with lots of color, sound and graphics, and because the 99/4A was designed to work with a speech synthesizer. I slipped the cartridge-type program into the machine, turned up the volume, and asked our guests to come in.

Kathy headed straight for the microcomputer. She stood listening and watching, a wide grin on her face, as the music played and animated graphics danced on the screen. A menu choice of routines appeared and I carefully reached in front of Kathy and pressed the key for letter identification. The screen changed, new music began and Kathy watched, eyes as big as saucers and glued to the screen. The synthesizer spoke everything on the screen. A letter appeared and the synthesizer spoke as the instructions appeared "Find the letter T." Kathy watched me carefully look to the keyboard for a match. I took each key, in the row, quietly shaking my head until I found the T. I took my finger to the screen and then to the keyboard and pressed the T. A colorful display with a musical jingle and reinforcement from the synthesizer told me I was right, and Kathy watched. The next letter was presented. This time I made a wrong choice, and the synthesizer encouraged, "No, try again." Looking carefully at the keys, I pressed the correct key and again received the color, music and synthesizer reward. I did this five times before Kathy made any indication that she wanted to try. Her hand reached for the keyboard just as I was about to push the key and I simply nodded my head and her finger pressed the key. Color, music, the voice, and a very big smile from Kathy. The next letter appeared and I waited for Kathy but Kathy seemed to be waiting for me. I started to raise my hand to the keyboard and she did the same. Together, we looked for a match but it was Kathy who found it and without hesitation pressed the key.

Kathy has her own microcomputer now. Her parents made the decision to buy one based on their sheer joy of the experience in our living room. Will the microcomputer help Kathy learn? I believe it will. How much she will learn, to what degree this tool may influence her development, is still a wide-open question.

Comparatively little research has been done on microcomputer technology for the mentally handicapped. However, what little has been done shows great promise. A recent project conducted by the University of Wisconsin-Stout, under the direction of Sam Jenkins, tackled the relation, if any, between standard IQ and an ability to use the computer keyboard.

The research took place at Indianhead Enterprises, a center for the developmentally disabled in Monomonie, WI. IQs of the participants ranged from 30 to 88. The Texas Instrument 99/4A home computer was used in conjunction with the computer's speech synthesizer. The program used displays a model of the TI keyboard on the screen and randomly flashes keys on and off. The object is to drill the student on the key locations. The computer automatically tallies the student's responses for later analysis. The student receives immediate feedback through the audible synthesizer as each key is pressed.

Five people were selected for a brief pilot study to iron out procedural difficulties. After the pilot group was run through the experiment, all thirty students took part.

Each student was given five minutes on the task. Performance on the task ranged from 100 percent correct to zero correct. In some instances, students with higher IQs did not do as well as some with lower IQs. Statistically, the correlation between IQ and performance on the research task was not significant. Indeed, it was not even particularly strong.

Of this project, Jenkins stated:

> *Our interpretation of the results is that IQ measures per se are not adequate in judging whether a retarded student could interact with a computer assisted instruction program via the microcomputer keyboard. Further research is suggested from these results. We are currently finishing a follow up study which investigates the effect of training on the student. We provided short sessions of training to the student where he had the opportunity to practice using the keyboard followed by a test period. The data have not been analyzed but our clinical observations suggest that simple verbal prompts and encouragement from a trainer greatly aids the student in learning the correct keystrokes. This is consistent with our general experience in working with the mentally retarded on computer exercises. Simple, commonsense assistance can be extremely helpful to the learner.*
>
> *In any case, the response of the student to the experience is almost always positive. The students seem to be very motivated by the sight and sounds of the computer exercise. They seem to focus their attention much better and for longer periods of time than is normally observed on other learning exercises. The nonverbal cues such as facial expression, verbal explanations, etc., all suggest that great excitement and joy was experienced by the participants.*

News of a project launched by the Association for Retarded Citizens of the United States, headquartered in Arlington, Texas, shows promise in another area of microcomputer technology. The project is looking at ways to use advanced technology to meet the most basic kinds of needs for the severely and profoundly mentally retarded through bioengineering.

About three-fourths of all institutionalized mentally retarded people function in the severe and profound range. The project director, Dr. Al Cavalier, commented, "While their developmental sequence is similar to nonretarded persons, their rate of development is much slower. A capacity does exist; they can learn, but teaching techniques which have proven to be beneficial to higher functioning mentally retarded persons have failed in many instances with this group. Answers may lie in advanced technology."

The new approaches to be used in Dr. Cavalier's project will draw on the principles and technology of biomedicine, rehabilitation engineering, the aerospace and computer fields, psychology, special education and other disciplines. It would appear the project is the first effort coordinated to bring all these disciplines and microcomputer technology together to solve problems for the severely mentally retarded. Among the project goals will be included the development of many new devices such as a reduced gravity device that could adjust the amount of body weight supported by a multiple handicapped person to strengthen muscles used in walking upright and improve coordination, biotelemetry devices to accentuate subtle bladder/bowel sensations while toilet training is in progress, and automated memory devices contained in a wristwatch or belt buckle that will "speak" a sequence of instructions for accomplishing a task.

Not all will be first-time inventions. A major aspect of the project will be the adaptation of existing technology that was developed for other uses. Electronic communication boards and voice synthesizers, for example, are planned as part of the project. The devices have not yet been adapted for widespread use by retarded people, and the bioengineering advisory committee sees great potential there.

When completed, this project could have widespread effects on the delivery of technology to this population. The final phase is designed as a nationwide sharing of information about the project results, and will involve audiovisual and written materials.

The implementation of microcomputers in the classrooms of the mentally handicapped is no different than any other educational application. Software that meets the need of the child, entertains, motivates and provides a learning experience is just as relevant for these children as for any other group, perhaps more so. The microcomputer is a very patient tutor and can deliver a given task at the learning rate of the student, again and again.

In an article published by *Closing The Gap*, researcher Jenkins of Wisconsin-Stout states:

> *Never before has the average person had such powerful tools to help overcome the deficits of retardation. The microcomputer represents a welcome addition to the "home teaching staff." I have seen enthusiasm and immediate acceptance of the microcomputer as I work with individuals and their families to address learning needs. For the retarded*

person who is able to take control of this powerful technology (and isn't any computer interaction, no matter how simple, a situation of operator control?), this is often a novel and exhilarating experience. Time and time again, I've seen the joy in the face of a retarded learner as he succeeds at a "mental" task and receives the recognition from the machine, his peers, and parents. I believe this is the essential reason that we humans of whatever level of ability find the microcomputer such a fascinating machine. We can succeed at our individual levels at mental tasks. This is inherently rewarding to us. In addition, we may be recognized by other people for our accomplishments. This is the most powerful reward of all!

The development of special interactive devices such as light pens and touch-sensitive screens may well have applications with the mentally handicapped unable to use the conventional keyboard. These devices are part of the arsenal of peripherals that assure some method of access to the computer for all children.

Special software that addresses the specific needs of retardation is being developed. Survival-skill software such as that developed by MCE, a Kalamazoo, MI, firm, addresses such needs as money management, home safety, banking skills, job readiness, etc. In field studies with the trainable and educable mentally retarded, this software which runs on the Apple II and IIe demonstrated the useability of microcomputer software with this population. Eight students, ages twelve to fifteen with an IQ range of 32 to 47, used a program called "Poison Proof Your Home." The study showed a minimum growth of 20 to 30 percent between pre- and post-test scores. There were four such separate studies with different software and groups of students and growth patterns ranged from 20 to 70 percent.

There seems little question that the use of microcomputers with the mentally handicapped is a viable method of teaching. We can also assume that the same motivational advantages of the microcomputer will apply. It remains to be determined if learning will occur faster or lead to better retention.

Much needs to be done to determine how effective the discovery learning techniques of Logo might be with this group. So little is known about how these children learn. Perhaps if we allowed them the opportunity to demonstrate, through their own ability to explore an environment on their terms, we would learn a great deal more about how their information is received, processed and integrated into useable knowledge.

So much effort, of teachers and parents alike, is spent teaching to the handicap instead of to the learning ability. The "teaching" to the weakness looks for defects rather than strengths. Often the parent or teacher looks to the strength as just something they don't have to worry about fixing. If just a little of that effort could be diverted to discovery of strengths, nurturing those strengths and letting them expand, the results could be much different.

As E. Paul Goldenberg said in *Special Technology for Special Children*, "Mental retardation is a term that refers, vaguely, to a low level of functioning. The notion that it is a unitary condition, 'the Cause' of the low level of functioning, is wrong, explains nothing, and impedes progress in the education of the mentally retarded."

Physically Handicapped

Of all the uses for today's microcomputer, those for the physically handicapped may be some of the most dramatic. As an environmental control device, to do the tasks the body cannot, the microcomputer represents a prosthetic tool.

But first, there must be access to the computer, and for the physically disabled the standard, out-of-the-box microcomputer may require modification.

Just turning the machine on (with the switch in the back) can present problems. Simple toggle switches that can be manipulated by the user and placed where they can be reached are a good starting place.

Another basic problem can be loading software into the disk drive. Low-cost ramps can be constructed to allow sliding the disk into position, up the ramp and into the drive, with a hand, head or mouthstick as the power source. For individuals unable to use the ramp method, a completely automated system, much like the old juke box record player system, can store and insert disks for the user.

Many educational and entertainment programs have been modified for single switch scan routine interaction. This means that the software has been modified to present a scan technique automatically. This allows the user to pick a choice from the screen by closing a single switch. Most of the modified software allows for user selected scan rate (how fast the cursor will move between choices) to allow for faster or slower reaction times of the user.

Sophisticated special software has been developed that will cover a wide range of special needs. Picture-Com, developed by Dr. Josej T. Cohn for the Apple II and IIe, is for the nonverbal, profoundly motor-handicapped who cannot read English. Both Bliss symbols and Pictograms are available and are presented on video screen pages with sixteen pictures per page. The user can create messages by choosing the pictures one by one; as this is done the English equivalent is printed at the bottom of the video screen.

A wide selection of educational software (see Appendices) has been adapted to scan routine with single or multiple switch interaction. There are even advanced types of software that allow user definable word and phrase dictionaries, calculator mode, telephone answering, dialing and directory service, and complete environmental control, all in one piece of software. For the severely disabled person, these types of "single switch" interactive routines can provide access to the microcomputer for basic communication needs, educational requirements and environmental control.

Scan routine software can be either programs written especially for use by the physically disabled or specially adapted programs. It is possible, however, to use *any* software if an interface can be made to emulate the keyboard. This would allow the user to access the computer in such a way that both the computer and the software function normally, as if they were not controlled by a special input routine. There are several approaches to providing this sort of transparent input. The common and more expensive methods are through actual keyboard emulators or with another microcomputer. Both provide very powerful and transparent interaction, but they are not cheap. If your microcomputer of choice happens to be an Apple II or IIe, however, there is another way.

An Adaptive-Firmware Card for the Apple II was developed by the Maplewood School Computer Project, of Edmonds, WA. Assistance for final development and dissemination was provided by the Trace Center's Commercial Facilitation Program, through several grants. This card provides a low-cost method that allows all software, including graphics and complicated spreadsheets like VisiCalc, to run using a variety of transparent input modes including scanning, Morse code and direct selection techniques. In addition to providing a method of keyboard input, the card will also simulate game paddles and switches.

The firmware card plugs into slot 7 of the Apple II and a small control box mounts on the side of the microcomputer. A thumbwheel switch on the box will allow selection of ten different input modes, while the normal keyboard also remains active.

The ten different input modes provide access to any software. A severely disabled person can access the microcomputer software of choice through the following:

One Switch Scanning: All input is handled through a single switch. Upon switch closure a group of letters and symbols will be presented at the bottom of the screen and the cursor will automatically scan at the rate previously set. The letters are arranged in groups and scanned. When a group is selected the cursor will scan the individual letters within the chosen group. The letters are arranged so that the most-used letters are easiest and fastest to reach. Although all of the selections are displayed on the screen, they do not alter the contents of the screen, thereby allowing any software to be used.

Step Scanning: All input is controlled through a single switch. However, this routine differs in the way the cursor moves across the letter choices. The cursor does not scan at a preset rate but instead requires that the switch be closed repeatedly to advance the cursor. Once a selection has been made, there is a delay (user selectable) before the cursor is ready for the next selection. Again the switch is closed, repeatedly, to advance to each available selection. This method is designed for individuals unable to handle the precise timing required for one switch scanning.

Inverse Scanning: This is one switch scanning in reverse. In this routine, the user holds the switch closed to scan and releases to select.

Morse Code 1: Just as the name would imply, the input mode is Morse Code. Operating from a single switch, the "dots" and "dashes" (short and long switch closures) are signals sent to the computer to represent letters and control keys of the keyboard. This routine can be much faster than the scan techniques if the user has or can develop the necessary muscular control. The system uses the standard International Morse Code and a number of additional codes to allow full access to the Apple II.

Morse Code 2: This is a two switch input system that forms an automatic keyer. One switch sends dots and the other dashes. This mode also has a software memory buffer that allows the user to get ahead of the microcomputer; i.e., if a dash is sent before the last dot is finished, the firmware card will accept the entry.

Assisted-Keyboard: This input design helps the one-finger or headstick typist to type all shift and control codes. Two auxiliary switches provide the shift and control functions. Hitting the auxiliary control switch once allows the next character to be a control character, but following keystrokes will be unaffected. Hitting the control switch twice will lock the control mode and all subsequent key presses will be sent as control keys, until the auxiliary switch is activated again. A special mode is also provided that allows the repeat function.

Parallel Mode: When this option is used, the firmware card acts as a straight keyboard emulator. Any parallel ASCII (American Standard Code for Information Interchange) character received by the card through a parallel port will be entered into the computer as if it had been typed on the keyboard.

Serial Mode: As with the parallel mode, the card acts as a keyboard emulator. Any serial ASCII character fed to the firmware will be received as keyboarded data.

Specific Disabilities 61

Expanded Keyboard: This mode will support any 8- by 15-switch matrix.

Special options supported by the card include seven paddle modes. These allow the user to use a single switch instead of paddles to play games.

From the descriptions of this firmware, it is not hard to imagine the interface possibilities. Just about any physically handicapped individual can use the microcomputer through one or more of the option modes. This interface then allows a person the ability to access the entire software library that has been developed for Apple II microcomputers.

All of the extensive Apple educational programs become accessible to a physically handicapped child using this firmware card. The need to modify programs no longer exists. The child can use exactly the same software as his or her peers.

Today, it is reasonable to expect that access to the microcomputer can be attained by even the most severely physically handicapped. The educational, recreational and life-skill software that has been referred to so often in these pages can be used just as effectively by this population. The microcomputer and peripherals such as the Apple firmware card bring all of the uses of the computer to the physically handicapped because, once access to the computer has been accomplished, the means to control other software and devices has been achieved.

The very first edition of *Closing The Gap* (April/May 1982) included a story on a young Minnesota teenager named Roger. Roger lived unable to speak or do anything for himself, for he, like more than 10,000 children born each year, suffers from cerebral palsy.

Roger spent the first twelve years of his life unable to communicate, except by using pictures and symbols. He could indicate his needs by pointing a hand, over which he had little control because of the lack of muscle coordination.

When Roger was five, through the intervention of his foster family and his local community Head Start program, he learned the Bliss symbols and began to learn to read.

Homelife centered around Roger in his wheelchair, where his adopted family saw to his needs, entertained him and taught him. His chief educational environment was the residential school where he attended classes and received occupational and physical therapy.

Difficulty in communication was Roger's biggest burden, beyond his physical limitations. Even after the addition of his Bliss "sight" method of talking, his communication attempts were arduously slow and as in all such situations, prone to inaccuracies by those attempting to interpret his communication.

Then a wonderful thing happened. Dr. David Seyfried, a true pioneer in practical use applications for the microcomputer, was able to get the local school district to loan Roger a computer for the summer. Dr. Seyfried and his staff modified standard drill-and-practice educational software to scan routine and the educational enrichment of Roger's life began.

At the very center of Dr. Seyfried's involvement in the project was the desire to bring communication skills to Roger. The method eventually used consisted of 983 memorized figures, letters and words that corresponded to numbers. With the use of the scan technique, Roger was able to choose numbers that corresponded to his vocabulary choice. The system also supported the ability to spell out proper names or words not included in the base vocabulary. The chosen numbers are then converted to a written message on the screen. Through a single switch closure (in this case a large disk-switch mounted on Roger's wheelchair tray) Roger was able to begin written language communication for the first time.

Added to the system was a beeper that replaced the bell for attracting the attention of family or staff to tell them a "message" was waiting. Later, a speech synthesizer was added, giving Roger his first controlled speech. Writing letters became a reality, too, when a word processing program and printer were added to the system.

The microcomputer (Apple II) and all of these things that changed Roger's life so dramatically took place in 1980. Yet today, the number of cerebral palsy victims interfaced with a microcomputer is shamefully low. The systems available today do not require special software as was the case with Roger's communication program, for it and many other electronic Bliss systems are available. As discussed earlier, it is no longer necessary to modify educational software to scan, since the emulators and firmware cards do this already.

Dr. Seyfried summed up what today's technology has meant to Roger and what it should mean to all physically handicapped children and adults in his article "Where Do We Go From Here" in *Closing The Gap* (April/May 1982):

> The recent ability of Roger to use a microcomputer benefits all people who have occasion to communicate and to interact with him and other nonverbal individuals. For example, Roger's parents or others in charge of his well-being no longer have to constantly be in the same room with him to ensure that his needs are met. Instead, all they have to do is to be close enough to hear the alert of a persistent beeping from the computer which informs them that there is a "message waiting." When the beeping sound is heard anyone within hearing distance can simply go to the

computer and see or even hear Roger's message as it is displayed or actually spoken by the computer.

Roger's audience has now increased from the audience of four or five well-trained people who could read his specialized eye-pointing communication system to an infinite audience consisting of anyone who can read or understand spoken language. The benefits of a mind and the experience of a boy with a voice locked inside his body have suddenly become freed to communicate with virtually anybody.

The microcomputer is giving the minds of severely physically handicapped people like Roger the opportunities for expression and "intellectual mobility" that the wheelchair and orthopedic prothesis have given to their bodies. Roger can now speak, do math, social studies, or science with total independence. Indeed, the microcomputer can truly be considered a "communication prothesis." The immediate question that we must ask is: "how do we get these prostheses (microcomputers) to everyone like Roger?"

I have personally spent hundreds of man hours researching and developing Roger's computerized verbal and printed communication program. The reward for my efforts was immediately forthcoming when almost immediately after Roger began using the computerized communication system in his home, when he entered the number 003 by means of a special switching device which I constructed. He then made a strained effort to focus his eyes upon me while his message appeared on the computer screen. I will never forget that moment or the message.

Where will Roger go from here? We know for sure that his path won't be blocked by his inability to communicate to an infinite audience. As I mentioned earlier he has already given the world one of the most beautiful messages of his life. That message was 003 which was of course .... THANKS.

Individuals with spinal cord injury, muscular dystrophy, anyotrophic lateral sclerosis or other similar conditions that prevent access to a standard keyboard may also look to voice entry systems. One of the first and most widely used systems is the Shadow/VET, for the Apple II, produced by Scott Instruments.

The Shadow/VET is a voice recognition system that permits the user to execute computer commands by simply speaking into a microphone. The system requires a brief training period and offers a 98 percent accuracy rate. Training is an important factor, so if Shadow/VET is properly trained, immediate recognition can be expected. The basic components are a microphone headset, a speech preprocessor, a Shadow-Cache interface board (which also allows independent keyboard operation), and a software diskette. A forty-word vocabulary may be developed, with the capability of calling in up to twenty-five alternate vocabularies by voice command. Vocabulary training, recognition, saving and recalling vocabulary sets are all available through the system.

Between adaptive switch and voice entry devices, microcomputer technology, and all that it offers for man, everything is there for the physically disabled. Because of the unique capabilities of the tool, it is essential that this technology reach these potential users. For children, I look to education, and the system that is in place (mandated by U.S. Public Law 94-142) to deliver both the tool and the training to use it most effectively. For adults, medical and vocational rehabilitation practitioners must gain the knowledge and prescribe technology as readily as they do aspirin.

The most perplexing part of the problem—that gaining the knowledge, "the know how"—is not in any way difficult. The "difficult" parts already have been done. Apple Computer Company, Inc. and all the other computer companies have invented, marketed and brought the microcomputer to the public. Scott Instruments, Street Electronics Corporation and organizations like them have developed the peripherals. Literally thousands of software publishers have brought their products to market. It's all sitting there, waiting to be used. The only hurdle left is getting the information about how this technology can benefit the handicapped into the hands of the public and to somehow make them understand how easy it really is to implement. If we can do that, there will never be another intellect, trapped in a body, unable to communicate.

Logo

IV

So far, this book has covered the microcomputer primarily as a *teaching* tool and as a prothesis for handicapped children. These are important uses of this technology, to be sure, but the computer is much more than has been described because it also is a tool of *learning*.

Teaching a child a certain set of academic goals, (math facts, for example) is one thing. To impart the thinking and problem solving skills needed to use the math facts is quite another. It has long been the goal of education to do both. However, with handicapped children the "facts" part seems to get the lion's share of attention. Parents and educators alike seem to focus on the handicap and spend most of their available time teaching to the weakness and ignoring the strengths that may be there, to the point where the strengths may never be discovered, much less nutured.

"Learning" by doing, to manipulate an environment, to have meaningful control of that environment, to build, explore, express ideas and to build on those ideas, is an atmosphere foreign to most handicapped children. Their world is filled with pressures to overcome the disability, leaving little opportunity for self-expression or intellectual stimulation. The very children who need self-expression, an identification of self, are the ones most often deprived of the opportunity for that expression. It is common to have these children attack their own weakness with little or no effort directed toward the strengths. A well orchestrated army (the educational system) attempts to remove the weakness to the exclusion of everything.

I remember a well-meaning teacher who wanted my deaf son, Marc, to attend an additional hour of speech during his physical education time. Marc excels at sports and dearly loved the opportunity to show that he excelled. It was the one time in the school environment where he viewed himself as an equal, where he could develop and protect his self image. I am sure the teacher's intentions were the very best, but teaching to the weakness, not the whole person, was her specialty, and like so many specialists, she failed to recognize all the needs of the child. It is this obsession with the handicap, to the exclusion of other things, that deprives handicapped children of intellectual expansion and self-expression.

The microcomputer and the use of a language called Logo can offer a "learning environment" and self-expression to all children, but especially to handicapped children. Logo is a philosophy of education. It was created in 1968 as part of a National Science Foundation research project. As a language, Logo has been under constant development. Most of the work since 1968 has been done at the Massachusetts Institute of Technology (MIT) in the Artificial Intelligence Laboratory. However, significant contributions have been made by Bolt, Beranck & Newman, Inc., as well as a number of other universities. From 1968 until 1979, Logo was available only on large computer systems. In 1979, however, the MIT Logo Group began to adapt Logo for microcomputers.

Two adaptations were created. The first was for Texas Instruments, Inc. and the TI 99/4 microcomputer. The other was developed for the Apple II computer. The two systems are very similar. The TI version was created under the supervision of Seymour Papert while the Apple system was supervised by Harold Abelson.

Logo, as a philosophy, allows children to interact with the microcomputer as a learning tool; that is, to be in charge of the environment and to create in self-directed ways rather than just reacting to preprogrammed tasks.

The focus for this new environment is Turtle Geometry or Turtle Graphics, using a small triangular cursor that is controlled by the user. The turtle can move in four ways: forward, back, right and left. From these four commands the user discovers the infinite number of movements under his or her control. Distance is controlled by adding a number to the directional command: Forward 50 moves the turtle fifty turtle spaces or steps. Turning right or left is controlled in the same manner, with the entry of the degrees of the desired turn used as the command. Right 90 effects a turn ninety degrees to the right and sets the turtle for his next distance move.

Any series of commands can be written into what is called a *procedure*. This can be a list of commands to affect any geometric design by having the turtle leave a trail as it moves across the screen. Once defined as a procedure and given a name, the original design can be recalled by simply telling the turtle to draw the named procedure.

The discovery learning environment of Logo provides endless opportunities for investigation and expression. The child is the teacher. The computer knows nothing except the four basic commands. Unless the child tells the computer what to do, it does nothing. Everything the turtle does is under the control of the child, even to using his or her own vocabulary as "names" for the procedures created. The computer becomes an environment under the child's direct control, in movement, in language used and in directing the turtle's activities. This allows the child to build on the experiences encountered. There is no "right" or "wrong" in Logo. There is just "learning" when the turtle or procedure doesn't do what you expect it to do.

Logo has the ability to stimulate thought processes and logical sequencing. As the child moves the turtle and plans the desired destination of the next move, an ability to understand cause and effect emerges. The cause may not achieve the desired effect, but that becomes part of the learning process. Adjusting the commands, the sequence of the commands and the elements used may deliver the desired effect. The discovery process is at work and the child is given the opportunity to develop these very elusive skills.

Freedom from imposed constraints of the mind is the Logo environment's strongest feature. The child is free of the rituals of right and wrong. There is room to explore, expand and express when in control of the turtle. There is no "lesson" or prescribed way, only the free expression of the child's creativity. The structure is there but the child is able to build freely within the structure and without unnecessary limitations imposed by the structure.

The genius of Seymour Papert, Harold Abelson, Paul Goldenberg and the many others who created and developed Logo and those involved with the MIT microcomputer versions of the language have given the educational system an extremely powerful children's language for the computer. This language has now left the controlled research environment and has moved to the hands of those who are working with children on a day-to-day basis.

Oddly enough, most of that effort seems to be in the private sector, not in education. Two examples come to mind. One is the Young Peoples LOGO Association in Richardson, Texas under the direction of founder, James H. Muller and The Family Computer Center, in Northfield, Minnesota operated by Griff and Robbie Wigley. These two centers (and there are many more) operate outside of public education but their efforts center on bringing Logo to children in the purest form—that of the intended "learning environment."

Logo is just beginning to gain popularity within the educational system. As the price of personal microcomputers comes down, the ability to add this "learning language" to the school curriculum becomes reasonable. However, an understanding of the Logo philosophy is critical if proper use of the language is to develop. There is the danger of adding Logo to a classroom and using it like a lesson-based "right-wrong" activity.

Griff Wiggly, in a story for *Closing The Gap*, February/March 1983, points out the dangers but also gives some suggestions on how proper use of Logo in a classroom can be easily effected.

> *After giving students the Logo commands for forward, back, left and right, we ask them to explore the commands to see if they can figure out how to move the turtle where they want it to go. We think it is important to "not" ask the type of questions that are usually thought of as helpful. Examples of these "teacher pleaser" questions are "Does the turtle move forward when you say 'right 45'?" or "Who's discovered how to make the turtle do a square corner?" This approach typically conveys to the students that what's important is the right answer to the teacher's questions and who gets it first. The students who answer correctly are seen to be "smart" and therefore learning. The philosophy of Logo is to create an environment in which students are learning for learning's sake. While it may be clear that "teacher pleaser" questions may be a put down to students who aren't skilled at answering them, they also do a disservice to the students who do. They will be fooled into thinking they are good learners when they are actually only learning something temporarily to please or impress another.*
>
> *As an alternative, consider the following statements: "Notice the difference between right 45 and forward 45." "Explore what happens when the turtle goes off the edge of the screen." "Try a square, triangle, or a letter of the alphabet if that interests you." These statements allow room for exploration and discovery without introducing elements of competition and "teacher pleasing" that inhibit all students. If you wish to explain a certain concept then go ahead and explain it without the questions. "Here's another way to do it." Or if you are too ingrained to stop yourself from asking "teacher pleaser" questions, at least tell your students that you do not want answers to the next series of questions—just to think about the answers to themselves.*

Using Logo for its intended purpose—creating a learning environment—is going to require some deviation from the tried and true educational concepts most educators use. The changes are subtle, but very important if the true strength of Logo is to stay intact in today's educational setting. Those who take the time to understand Logo will find it a motivating, ingenious method of teaching problem solving skills through learning. A child given such a tool can develop to the extent of his or her ability because there is no limit, just building blocks of knowledge with which to expand to yet another step beyond.

James H. Muller, founder and president of Young Peoples' LOGO Association, Inc., said it this way. "The real genius of Logo is that young people can start with their everyday vocabulary—the form of expression with which they are most familiar—and move into a totally new audio visual realm where they can explore, experience, discover—and learn the fundamentals of geometry, math, text manipulation and a host of other opportunities. It doesn't matter if this is 1882, 1982 or 2082. Unless the functioning of the human brain changes drastically, the fundamentals of learning will remain the same. With Logo you break a problem down into the component elements with which your experience will allow you to work, and then you use these elements to procedurally discover new knowledge. In essence, you start with the known and move to the unknown."

As the educational use (in schools) of Logo increases, one can only hope that a true Logo implementation will occur. Like so much of the educational computer use to date, there is the danger that improper and incomplete use will be allowed to flourish. The idea that education—"the system"—cannot change to accommodate microcomputer advancements like Logo has been expressed by many people. I prefer to believe that the problems preventing change are temporary, more a lack of information and overall understanding and not caused by a system permanently incapable of change. Some would argue that our educational system has become too embedded in an immovable bureaucracy, insensitive to the needs of the population it was designed to serve. This may be the case with some of the federal and state administrative bodies that are supposed to be "leading" education. However, I find the on-line teachers ready for change. As we do teacher training workshops around the country, it becomes obvious that "the tail is wagging the dog," and that the teacher in the classroom is ready to deliver technology to the population and will seek the information and training necessary, with or without the support of the bureaucracy.

Logo represents a language for the microcomputer that children can use like a set of building blocks. Because of the technology, these are not the stationary, solid cubes manipulated with hands. The blocks of Logo are intellectual blocks of learning from which other blocks can develop. As a child builds a "block" such as a procedure to draw a circle, he or she then has the ability to use that circle as expression. Having the turtle draw the circle as directed is one expression. Drawing the circle as part of other expressions is "building blocks of knowledge" in action. As an example: Joey, my nine-year old, made his first circle by copying the procedure from a Logo manual. Joey had observed the turtle's ability to draw a circle by watching his brother and sister. He wanted a procedure of his own on his own disk, to do the same thing, so he went about it the only way he had available at the time—the manual. He was busy copying the procedure into the computer when I walked into the room. The procedure in the manual reads:

```
TO CIRCLE2   :SIZE
REPEAT 360 (FORWARD   :SIZE RIGHT 1)
END
```

"Mom, will the turtle make a circle if I tell him to turn left instead of right?," he asked. "I don't know, Joey," I replied, "Why don't you try it." He returned to the machine and said, "I hope so because I don't want to use the same circle as Marc (his brother)." Joey completed his "left" procedure and tried it. To his delight it worked just fine. Joey went on to use his special circle to create a picture library of things that were important to him. His expressions, using the building block of his circle were endless. There was the "snowman" picture that took a great deal of thought because of the placement of the circles and the pen-up movement of the turtle before the next circle was drawn. There were faces, even flowers using the circle and lines to effect the appearance of standing arrangements.

Joey's choice of expression happened to be pictures he could draw with the few procedures he had taught the turtle to execute. He was content to explore the relationship of size to space, to create from within using his artistic imagination as a stimulus for the problem solving skills he was developing in order to execute his pictorial ideas.

This example is just one of the hundreds of uses Logo provides, because it is just one child's use. If you looked at two children using Logo, you would find two uses, a hundred children, a hundred uses. Each child will explore Logo and find something new because it is not a lesson to be taught, it is discovery of the unknown. Every child will receive something unique from the Logo environment because it is the child's own environment, created and taught to the microcomputer by the child.

Logo is far more than the turtle graphics talked about here. It is a procedural language capable of combining commands into procedures and using those procedures as stepping stones for other procedures. The steps may be one of the primitive Logo commands or any user-defined procedure. Logo also can be used as an interactive programming language.

Much of the true value of the microcomputer for handicapped children will surface only if its uses follow the same philosophy of Logo. The microcomputer can provide discovery learning, as a tool with no threshold and no ceiling, one that gives the power of expression. Logo provides this in its purest form. However, uses by the handicapped child of telecommunication, word processing and speech synthesis can also provide the ability for discovery learning and self-expression. It is the combining of all these elements that will make the microcomputer a true prothesis for the intellectual and emotional development of the handicapped.

Logo is becoming available for all popular microcomputers. It should be made clear that certain versions have advantages over others and some have features that others do not. Appendix F has a list of the different versions for different brands and a brief description of the features each has to offer. The same appendix lists books and resources that will aid you in discovering Logo and the philosophy that is so essential for proper implementation.

Communication
V

Communication via microcomputer already is a major part of business and industry in this country. It would be very hard to live one day without having communications via computer touch our lives. Go to the grocery store or dial the telephone even once and you have been a part of communication via computer. In the grocery store, the bar code reader at the check-out counter is a means of inventory and price control that is done entirely by computer. When you dialed the telephone, you interfaced with a computer that took the number you dialed and connected you to your party. If the call was long distance, the computer timed the call, checked the rate to be charged, and communicated that information to another computer in the billing department. When you get your bill, there it is, all listed for you by computer: the number you called, how long you were connected to your party and how much you were charged for the privilege.

All communication by computer is accomplished by means of opening and closing switches. If an individual is communicating with a microcomputer using a typewriter-style keyboard, he or she is opening and closing switches for each letter or numeral that is typed into the machine. Each time the switch is activated a signal is sent to the computer. This signal is sent in a code on the binary numbering system—1s and 0s. Each letter, number, space, etc. is assigned a value based on a combination of 1s and 0s and this convention is standard between almost all computers, including microcomputers.

Programs are stored on disk or tape in the same fashion—a series of 0s and 1s arranged in code to be sent to the processor within the computer for translation to an output device.

The output can be to the screen, to a printer for permanent copy, to a speech synthesizer, or to a modem where tones of sound representing the ASCII code can be sent over telephone lines.

It is this common binary language of computers and the ability of translation by the computer to the many different output modes that makes communication via microcomputer so very important. The speed, accuracy and versatility of converting communication to a chosen method of output is what the information age is all about.

On-Line Services

On-line services are best described as a means of accessing information of choice via telecommunication, microcomputer and modem communication over telephone lines. With a microcomputer and modem you are able to contact large computer data banks and access that information at will for personal or professional use. This can be done from the convenience of home, school or office, by having your microcomputer dial the number of the on-line service, establish a connection and, under your direction, communicate with the large data banks for information you want. This is widely done in business and industry as a method of quick and easy access to the most current data available on any given subject.

The area of information can be anything, current events for instance. There are several on-line services that are general in nature and among their long lists of services include several electronic editions of daily newspapers around the country, major wire services, AP (Associated Press) or UPI (United Press International). With a "one word search" it is possible to pick up all the stories filed about a subject, let's say "deafness." By telling the system, through menu choice and that "one word," you can search the system for all news stories filed on the subject of deafness carried on the wire service that day. Perhaps you want to know what has been filed in the last week—all you have to do is tell the system what you want. On this same "general" on-line service there are over two hundred different subject categories: weather, aviation, fashion, travel, government publications, movie reviews, shopping, electronic editions of magazines, education, personal computing services, financial services, banking by computer, and E-mail (Electronic Mail). The list could go on and on and this is just one of hundreds of on-line services.

The key element here is that these services are accessible by anyone with a microcomputer, modem and telephone service. A person may be physically handicapped, able to access the computer with only a single switch closure device, but that person also can access the service. Remember the keys are just switches for on and off. Any switch will do the same thing. The universal language of 0s and 1s allows any input device to be used and any output device to be selected. The communication is being accomplished by the processor inside the microcomputer with the 0s and 1s from your computer talking to the 0s and 1s of the remote computer. The microcomputer will accept any method of turning on and off switches. It will also convert those 0s and 1s to any form of output device: printer, voice synthesizer, etc. Suddenly the communication capability of the microcomputer, with its 0s and 1s, is extended to handicapped individuals in a way only dreamed of a few years ago. From the confines of a wheelchair, with only one reliable means of closing a switch to unlimited access to information, this person can now shop, bank, use an electronic library, do research, send and receive E-mail, play games, review commodity and stock market information, use any information and send any information of choice, and do so by closing a switch.

The communication capabilities of the microcomputer are the base for the "information age" or "computer revolution" that is changing our society. These changes in the way an entire society will transmit and receive information happen to meet the needs of handicapped individuals very well. The lack of mobility to go to an information source, the inability to hear audible information, ineffective or nonexistant speech ability, etc., are not restrictive conditions to communication via microcomputer. As more progress is made in converting our society to the "information age" the more access the handicapped individual will have. Because handicapped individuals have much more incentive to use microcomputers than the rest of the population, handicapped individuals actually will be entering this new age with an advantage. The "isolation" that has been so synonymous with "handicap" can, to a large degree, be removed. Equal access to information and the ability to interact with it, communication via microcomputer, are one in the same.

The list of uses for on-line services, communication via microcomputer, includes convenience shopping. Today, as the numbers and kinds of shopping available on computer increase almost daily, it is easy to see how this new way to "buy" will influence handicapped individuals. A friend of mine told me the story of a man he viewed as the worst dressed individual he had ever met. It wasn't that the person could not get to stores to shop but that when he got there he could not interact with the store clerks. He wore pants that were too big, shirts of weird colors and even shoes that didn't fit because every time he went into a store, he would grab the first thing available. He had a stutter, and rather than attempt communication with the clerk, he simply bought what was on display regardless of color or fit.

What is called "convenience shopping" available for society in general may well be the "only" shopping ability for some members of that same society. As more and more of the buying habits of the masses turn to microcomputer-based shopping, so shall it be for the handicapped population. They will then have the same access, perhaps the only access they have ever had, to purchase products the same way as everyone else.

The information available by use of on-line services includes many educational opportunities. Without going to the commonly talked about "school without walls" concepts that may well be in our futures, it is possible to use the state of the art to enhance education as we know it today.

Many of the general information on-line services commonly subscribed to by the public contain electronic encyclopedias. Just like the bookshelf variety, they are a reference library of information, but they can be accessed by microcomputer and modem. The search techniques are the same in that you must know what you want to look up but instead of flipping pages to find the subject, you let the computer find it. Type in the word or subject and the computer goes to its data bank and places the information on the screen. Faster? Yes! As complete as the bound book variety? Yes, and in most instances, more so, because the ability to update the information to its most current status is inherent in electronic versions. What is current events today will be in the encyclopedia tomorrow. It is an on-going, continually updated, reference library available at your finger tips, anywhere, anytime.

Encyclopedias are but the tip of the iceberg in electronic reference libraries available today. Complete law libraries, medical and technical data of all varieties are available. These services make information gathering a very simple procedure. Research can be done from the classroom, home or office electronically rather than in the dusty aisles of an obscure section of the library.

The convenience, speed and timeliness of gathering information in this way is having a profound effect on society. Today, a major law firm would be considered in the dark ages if it were unable to use electronic information gathering and research techniques. Medical, technical, financial, scientific and engineering institutions are also well on the way to integrating computer communications and on-line data banks into their research procedures.

A form of on-line information called timeshare (communications via main-frame to dumb terminal) is actually how education began using computers. There have been many main-frame on-line services that were designed to provide courseware, direct interactive materials for students. Those were the days of timeshare units which were centrally located large computers interacting with terminals in the schools. The age of the microcomputer has changed that timeshare concept, however. Organizations such as MECC (Minnesota Educational Computing Consortium) began as a source of timeshare educational materials for students. There were large computers in the central location and schools paid both membership and phoneline charges to access the computers, much as the on-line services for microcomputer do today.

MECC began developing microcomputer software almost immediately after the first microcomputer was introduced, and MECC's support of both hardware and software for the microcomputer literally put the timeshare computers out of business in Minnesota. The case of the well-known PLATO system from Control Data was much the same story. Their timeshare concept had to give way to the creation of the same courseware on microcomputer disk in order to sell the product.

There are many reasons for the move to microcomputers in education but two seem to stand out as the major factors: flexibility and price. With a microcomputer you have the same on-line capability as with the dumb timeshare terminals, and in addition you have a machine that can run software from many sources, as well as one you can program or adapt for personal use. With the cost of personal computers so low and going lower, there just is not any reason to tie to a single source of information such as the original timeshare concepts required.

One way to look at the on-line capabilities of microcomputers is that you have the ability and the personal flexibility to tie to any timeshare system you choose and still have a personal machine to do your bidding which is a rather powerful combination as a tool of education. There are actually two educational uses of on-line services available through microcomputers. There is the opportunity for direct student use which can be called instructional and the professional use which can be called career enrichment.

Instructional Services

There can be no question that telecommunications as an instructional device is going to have a profound effect on the handicapped. The ability to access information from anywhere at any time and to have choice of output (speech, Braille, screen, or printer) gives mobility to the mind. If a student is unable to get to the original information, for whatever physical reason, the information can still be there through telecommunications. Just the understanding that on-line information can be brought to the physically handicapped is staggering, but to realize that any nonreader can have this information through speech synthesis, that the deaf can have it on the screen or from a printer, or that the blind can have it in Braille or speech brings the real world to the handicapped. Any of the research, educational or instructional data stored across the country can be brought to the classroom and to the individual microcomputer used by the student.

On-line data banks, accessible by microcomputer, are much like having libraries of information at your fingertips. I am sure it wouldn't take long for a social studies teacher to use telecommunication and on-line data to demonstrate the influence of communication on society on any subject such as finance or the stock market, for instance. The quotations are on-line just a few minutes after the transactions take place. Instead of a textbook description, the classroom activity could be watching the market change minute by minute via microcomputer.

Education has been teaching through books that simulate the real world because it was impossible to bring the world into the classroom. The strategy used to establish a learning environment usually includes lectures, study guides, films, library research, independent study projects, which all involve the students in problem solving and information gathering types of activities. The real world is using telecommunications and on-line data for real life applications of these same learning techniques. Education, it would seem, will have to make the move to teaching with the tools the students will be expected to use after their school years. Information gathering, library research, independent study projects all will be computer-based activities for even the college age student of today when he enters the job market. The tools to integrate the real world into the classroom are there. Again, the barrier is not cost but one of informing and training the educator to use the technology of today.

Instructional uses of the microcomputer as a device of modern communication will make classrooms different in many ways but not in basic teaching strategies. Teachers that provide sound problem solving techniques to their students will find the microcomputer and modem an enhancement to the educational toolbox, a better hammer.

Successful use of communications via microcomputer as part of today's education is simple. Just use the computer as the tool it was designed to be. Use a modem to get outside the classroom and let the real world in. Allow the students to use the microcomputer as more than an electronic textbook. Let them use it for more than the drill-and-practice programs that are just another way of testing to see how well the teacher is getting the "facts" across.

For the handicapped child, a microcomputer, communications software and a modem can be the *entry* into the real world. Society is already well into the "information age" in a very practical sense. Most of business and industry conduct their data communication by computer. Suppose the educational environment for handicapped children included actual participation in the same sort of data exchange. Let's use electronic mail as an example. Today, electronic mail is fast becoming the standard for communication between individuals who desire instant, yet private communication of written materials. Allowing a child to set up "E-mail" communications capabilities could have some interesting ramifications. From a strictly educational point of view, there is the actual "how to" sending and receiving E-mail as well as the written language experience of sending mail of any kind and both steps are necessary in learning how to communicate in the real world of today. The uses of E-mail go far beyond this, however. Think of the social development possibilities. Friends across the country with the same interests and being able to exchange information with a number of different people are learning experiences in themselves, and for the handicapped child it is far more. Those communications are conducted from the microcomputer terminal, thereby giving this opportunity to a blind child as well as one who may be physically disabled.

The opportunity is there for the deaf and hearing impaired as well as non-vocal or language handicapped children. It can mean less isolation and more opportunities for interaction with others, outside the confines that the handicap induces. The universal translator of binary code to a choice of common but different outputs, combined with telecommunication, gives a freedom to the minds of these children. Through the microcomputer they can travel out of seclusion into the real world. The educational uses of this new-found freedom could include participation in all the uses the microcomputer has in our society. Banking, shopping, research, recreation, all the life skill areas could be learned through doing for real in the very way these children will be expected to function in just a few short years.

Of all the educational uses that present themselves through telecommunication, written language development is the most exciting. Now these children can leave the pencil and paper behind. In most cases the language difficulties are magnified when the tools for expression are pencil and paper. These children are faced with a struggle when a mistake is made and no options to correct it are available but erase or recopy. Communication software such as AE Pro (for the Apple II and IIe) has a very sophisticated text editing capability. This means that while using telecommunications (micro and modem) you have nearly the same type of text manipulation available as you would using a word processing program. Now the child can change a word or sentence with ease, and do so while preparing communication about to be sent over telephone lines to across the world if desired.

The other side of language development via telecommunication is what my husband and I call language with a purpose. This was discussed in Chapter III as it relates to our son. However, a little more on the subject is in order. The microcomputer and modem serve as a direct connect means to transmit written language. The effect is using the telephone lines for written language instead of voice communication. This can be done person to person just like a telephone or with another computer such as on-line services and bulletin boards.

For the child who has difficulty with written language, one-to-one communications via the computer and over telephone lines can be a reason to develop the skill. Through a desire and the model language that is displayed on the screen, children are able to experience two essential elements to learning: a reason for doing the task (personal communication directed to them personally provides motivation—language with a purpose) and a demonstration of how the task should be done (model language to emulate).

In practical application these two elements have far reaching effects on learning of any kind. Give a child a good reason and an example and chances are the teaching will expand to discovery learning. Written language or any skill, for that matter, is best learned by doing. With telecommunications, it is possible to offer the child an environment that gives both the reason and model from which to develop written language and to do so without the right/wrong concepts so destructive to anyone trying to overcome a handicap. Red correction marks on paper do little to stimulate learning if all they do is tell the child how wrong he is. Drills, especially lackluster ones without a motivational base except "please the teacher" are hardly the kind of routine that stimulates learning, especially if there is a better method.

Telecommunication offers so much to the learning environment because it provides activities that are interactive. The child sits down to the microcomputer and commands the system to dial a telephone number. This number could lead to direct communication with a friend or teacher, or to another computer without a live person on the other end such as a bulletin board. The other microcomputer answers the call. Now there is language on the screen. The called party identifies itself and the interaction begins: a one-on-one demand for written language. I can tell you this real-time demand for language creates an entirely different reason for the development of written language. It is a brand new element to consider in the teaching environment and a very positive one.

Much has been said and written about the social implications of microcomputers. Some say they will isolate people from one another and that they will change the way people interact. There will be change to be sure, but the entire integration of computers in society is based on their ability to communicate. The fact that they do it faster and cheaper than older methods is generally misunderstood. It frightens many people to think of information being transmitted between computers thousands of times faster than humans can think. But an important factor to remember is that a microcomputer is a machine created by man to do his bidding. The machine is nothing without man. A computer can do nothing without directions. Because the computer is a communicator, I see it as an asset to society, one that will enhance communication between all human beings.

The social implications of the microcomputer for the handicapped is a good example of the communication enhancement capabilities this technology brings. Talking to the rest of the world through the microcomputer brings a new freedom to the handicapped segment of our society. Their new ability to communicate will allow direct participation in the day-to-day activities of the world, instead of through second- and third-party interpretation. Their need for direct communication has always existed but only now are the tools available to allow this to happen.

The release from isolation that the microcomputer represents for the handicapped brings with it an ability to interact socially with the rest of society. This may well begin within the special interest groups that seem to grow up around microcomputers. There are vast numbers of clubs that form around specific brands of computers, both local and national. These clubs provide a forum for discussion, informational exchange and perhaps most important, an interaction of common interests. What is human interaction all about anyway? Isn't it finding common ground around which dialogue develops? This new extention, this ability to reach out beyond the confines the handicap imposes, is new ground for social development.

Clubs also form around professional, recreational and personal interests. These range from religion to politics and everything in between. The opportunities for communication through the microcomputer will enhance the opportunities the handicapped have to join in such dialogue. Communications of this type are growth-type experiences, both from an informational and social level. Exchanging ideas, being part of a discussion, on any subject, is part of what has been missing from the lives of many handicapped individuals.

Educational/Career Enhancement

Communication with telecommunications also offers the teacher, administrator, parents and handicapped individuals themselves the opportunity of informational exchange. Bulletin boards and data bases are coming on-line with forums designed specifically for educator use. One such service is BRS (Bibliographic Retrieval Services). BRS offers over fifty educational and professional data bases and bulletin boards through the service, six of which are listed under the subheading of education. Among the six is the School Practices Information Network and File (SPIN/SPIF). This particular data base provides current educational programs, practices and materials through a unit of BRS called the Education Service Group. Files contain such information as "The Nationally validated educational practices, State validated educational practices as identified by State Departments of Education through their Title IV-C programs, Special education programs and instructional materials, Teacher developed programs, school business practices, Curricula at all grade levels and in all subject areas, In-service programs and instructional software available for use with microcomputers."

As part of the microcomputer software file, there are more than 1,500 descriptions of courseware for all grade levels, major hardware types and content of the software itself in a review-type format. By using the "search" capability of the data base, it is possible to quickly identify software that is available in a specific subject area by describing the desired subject matter, hardware type, and grade level. The system does an instant search and pulls up the courseware description for you. In seconds you have retrieved information on availability and cost as well as content of the software.

SPIN/SPIF are accessed by membership fee, a per hour rate and royalty fee where applicable. Access to other BRS data (those other fifty data bases) is also available on a similar pricing structure; however the rate per hour and royalty fees vary greatly.

Costs of using a system like BRS are not that expensive, when compared to the cost of labor to do research. What would take hours of by-hand searching takes seconds by computer. A rate such as $18.00 per hour (the 1982 rate per hour for Pre K-12 public and private schools to access SPIN/SPIF) is within practical reach for most educational facilities.

BRS also offers an after business hours service called "BRS/After Dark." About the only thing that changes is the price charged for the service. A lesser membership fee ($50.00) and a greatly reduced per hour charge (in 1982 it was $6.00 per hour) makes the service affordable for individuals.

There are numerous national bulletin boards (some with membership fees) that provide communication and information, through public messages on the board, private E-mail and data base collections. One of the fastest growing services for educators is called *Special Net*. Its function is primarily to set up a network of communications between special education microcomputer users across the country that will allow members to communicate messages to the rest of the users. Another of this type (free use, however) is HEX (Handicapped Educational Exchange).

These types of bulletin boards make communication of information a very simple procedure. Instead of calling all your associates individually by telephone or mailing a letter or note to them, the bulletin board offers the convenience of posting an electronic message once on the board for all to see. Members (active ones anyway) review the board daily. Your message or information is there for all interested persons to see. This type of system is extremely useful, fast and cost-effective for all types of information exchange.

Communication is the very core of the computer revolution. The exchange of data by computer gives fast, timely and accurate transmission capability for any subject area and by any organization or individual. Reducing all data to a common code (binary 0s and 1s) is of course the secret. If more people understood how simple and useful communication by computer really is, I believe the "fear of the unknown" would diminish. I do not mean that users should be able to understand the language that makes the computer work; that is unnecessary. What is necessary to understand is that all things going into the computer (input), whether Braille, voice, typed or switch entry, are converted into the common language. Now that the microcomputer has received the common language it can do whatever the user wants it to do with that information. Since the computer is only looking at the common language, it can be commanded to put information out (output) in any form desired (typed, voice, Braille, screen or tone, etc.).

The common language of the microcomputer is enhancing the communications ability of man. Whatever else people may attribute to the computer, it is a communicator. It can be a communicator for individuals who need help transmitting and receiving information, and don't we all!

The Common Denominators
VI

Through the pages of this book, I found myself trying to convey a dual purpose for the microcomputer in special education. One role of this tool is the "special" needs side: using the microcomputer to bring equality to the handicapped child by meeting the special needs that may be present as a result of the handicap. These special needs may be met by special input or output devices or alternately by special software designed to perform a particular task. In either case the desired result is having the microcomputer help the child perform normal tasks that otherwise could not be done.

The other role of the microcomputer in special education is the common use side of the machine. These generally are the uses that all children have for the microcomputer: computer assisted instruction, drill and practice, word processing, telecommunication, etc.

Many of the uses that have been described are a combination of both special needs and the common uses of the microcomputer. Using typing tutors, for instance, is one example. Every child within the educational system today, able to use a standard keyboard, will be expected to interact with a microcomputer in that fashion. If they are going to learn to use this tool, they must learn typing skills. Is it proper to let elementary grade students "hunt and peck" and learn bad habits, or is it more appropriate to let them learn how to type from the start? Typing tutor software will have value for all children as a means to gain proper training to use the microcomputer. But for the learning disabled child, unable to write with paper and pencil, typing tutors will have even a greater meaning. Here a very common piece of software meets a special need as well as a general one.

Many common software selections can be termed "special need" software. Just as typing tutors serve a dual purpose, so will programs like word processing. These types of software are actually a requirement to meet the special needs of handicapped children and yet, after the "special" need is met, there remains the common need to use this software just as anyone would.

The educational uses of the microcomputer must include bringing a handicapped child in touch with ways to sidestep the handicap (the special needs) and then present the academic, social and entertainment uses (common needs) of this technology. With the microcomputer, the common and special needs can be met by the same machine. This means that a child unable to speak can be brought speech through the microcomputer. A very special need has been met, but now the use of that voice can include answering questions, and hopefully asking a few as well.

As a common denominator, the microcomputer will bring exciting activities to all people including the handicapped. The activities and interaction go far beyond the traditional education uses.

A project of the Minnesota Council on Quality Education brought the microcomputer into physical education. Recreational Education Alternative Curriculum Techniques (R.E.A.C.T.) designed and produced software products to help students learn refereeing skills and game strategies with the help of microcomputers. Archery, golf, bowling, skiing, sailing, along with the more common football, tennis, basketball, etc., are the subject of simulated game software designed to provide an understanding of the rules, skill principles and strategies of the sports. Students gain an understanding of the relationship between competition in a physical activity and competition strategies as well as a basic knowledge of the sport and rules governing the play.

A young high school student, weighing thirty pounds and confined to a wheelchair because of brittle bone disease, found the R.E.A.C.T. software a way to enhance his sports activity. He was able to engage in bowling and scuba diving but was unable to participate in games such as football or basketball. His interest in the contact sports was real but, because of the handicap, traditional participation was out of the question. His coach substituted actual playing of the game with R.E.A.C.T. simulation play and his expertise in those sports was able to grow. Within a few months he became so proficient at basketball strategy that the coaching staff added his talents to theirs as the official statistician for the team. For this young man the microcomputer was his entry into active participation in contact sports. Without it, his interest and skills could never have been able to flourish.

Simulations are very common types of software available for use in education. The subjects range from sports activities such as those of project R.E.A.C.T. to complex and dangerous scientific experiments as well as social studies demonstrations. With this software the microcomputer can become the science lab. Simulations of dangerous or expensive experiments can be conducted on the microcomputer, eliminating both the danger and cost factors but bringing the step-by-step learning experience to the students.

For the handicapped child, simulation software can bring a world of experiences that he or she would otherwise be unable to examine. An example is the science laboratory where acids and chemicals are needed for an experiment. A physically disabled child may not be allowed to participate for safety reasons—unable to handle the elements necessary for the experiment because he or she is unable physically to handle the apparatus. This same experiment can be simulated on the microcomputer, however, and the handicapped child indeed can participate.

As the educational uses of these kinds of software increase, the opportunities for handicapped children to access them also will increase. These simulations will enrich the learning experience because in many instances, without them, the opportunity for participation would not exist.

The common educational computer uses today remain primarily in the drill-and-practice area, but that is going to change. As the educational system is able to absorb the technology, curricula will change. As these curricula change to incorporate the microcomputer as the tool of access, the handicapped child will be able to move step for step with the mainstream population. The microcomputer will become the common denominator that allows handicapped children equality in education.

All children, but particularly handicapped children, need to use the microcomputer. They need it because it is a tool that can help them to learn. Far more important, it is the tool of the future. Society has embraced the microcomputer because it removes burdensome tasks and allows human beings an easier way of doing things. This is even more important for handicapped individuals because the number of burdensome tasks that the microcomputer can perform is greater for them than for any other population.

Once the special needs, the extra burdensome tasks, have been met by the microcomputer there are still the uses that everyone else has for the tool, and that is the common denominator factor that is so important.

If microcomputer technology is brought to handicapped children through the educational system now, and if that use encompasses the special needs—voice and communication for the nonvocal, Braille and speech synthesis for the blind, telecommunications for the deaf, word processing for all, including the learning disabled and new learning opportunities for the mentally handicapped—it is then possible for these children to address the multitude of other uses of this technology.

The influence of this machine extends beyond the educational environment. Obviously, the same kinds of equality that it brings to education can be extended into society in general. The job opportunities and the social and recreational pleasures extend to all people including the handicapped.

The pleasures of music and art, new forms as well as old, are being brought into the computer age. Music education is turning to the microcomputer as a teaching tool for compositional and performance control as well as drill and practice. Software exists that will compose one, two, three, even four or more voices simultaneously. It will play back those same voices as well as display all voices while the music is playing. Another allows each harmonic to be displayed as a three-dimensional graph. It also allows simultaneous manipulation of the three dimensions (time, amplitude and harmonic content) that go into creating synthesized sound.

There are programs that drill in melodic and harmonic intervals with any combination of interval sizes and qualities (major, minor, diminished, augmented and perfect) and practice in bass or treble clefs or the full staff. Ear training software exists that drills the aural recognition of diatonic chord progressions beginning with simple tonic/dominant root position chords to more complex patterns using all diatonic chords in root position and first and second inversion. Everything from simple sound identification of the degrees of the scale in game format to complex music composer programs are being used by musicians for teaching as well as original composition and performing.

The microcomputer as a paint pallet or sketch pad is also real. People such as Saul Bernstein, professor of classical art at California State University at Northridge, are leading the movement to blend the fine art of the masters into the graphic art of the microcomputer. Bernstein is famous in computer circles for his Einstein, Chaplin and Mozart computer paintings on the Apple. However, his acclaim in the world of television, winning the prodigious West award for excellence in educational broadcasting as well as a coveted Emmy, speaks to the recognition of microcomputer graphics as a new and viable art form.

Bernstein uses the microcomputer to investigate the classics. In a story that appeared in *Softalk*'s March 1983 edition, Howard A. Shore writes as he quotes Bernstein.

I even use the Apple to help teach my classes. It's especially effective when we're investigating the classics. Using computer technology, I trace the S curve along Eve's arm in this painting of Adam and Eve, by Peter Paul Rubens, and start the computer searching for other instances of that form. "Students are inclined to think that the old masters are irrelevant because they were realistic and are now old hat, so to speak." Even as he says this, the computer belies the students, outlining S curves as it finds them throughout the famous painting, proving the depth of meaning and abstraction in the artist of old. "The whole painting is composed of that one shape. The computer scans the painting and does a better job of finding the theme forms than I could. Since the computer does all the manipulations, I'm left free from any argument. I didn't do it; let them go argue with the computer. Well, it ends up that it's a terrific abstraction, relevant to their needs.

"It leaves the student in a quandary, doesn't it?" Bernstein chuckles. "In other words, I say, 'Here's the tape, take a look at it,' and then I just get out of their way."

Unimagined Forms. *A self-portrait by Rembrandt replaces the Rubens on the screen. The painting shows a full-face Rembrandt, but the computer sees more. Superimposed outlines bring out unimagined forms and devices.*

As you can see, the computer is finding a profile view superimposed with a three-quarter view. Not only did Rembrandt do this sort of thing, but Caravaggio before him, and Michelangelo before Caravaggio. Rubens, soon after Michelangelo, did it, too. In our own time, consider Pablo Picasso and Georges Braque.

Now the screen shows a computer-drawn silhouette entirely derived from lines found in the original face-on painting.

The students have seen something and they're provoked. Now they either say, "Well, the hell with it, I'm going to disregard it," which is going to hurt their education, or they have to go for it—which means they have to study the old masters. Therefore, I win," he laughs. "It's very devious. I'm using twenty-first century technology to explain seventeenth or eighteenth century painting."

As a creative device, an electronic canvas, Bernstein's work again sets the pace for a new art form. Again from the *Softalk* story, Shore writes:

> *Bernstein's work on an educational television show entitled* Needlecraft, *directed by Harry Ratner, won him the Emmy and the West awards in 1981. Now the Sony comes to life with his tape of the show.* "Needlecraft *was almost all done with the computer," he says over the musical opening. His pictures form and dissolve on the screen, counterpointing the music.* "All the transitions, the wipes, dissolves, everything, were done on the Apple II."
>
> *Because the Apple's output video signal is not directly recordable, Bernstein used the prototype video interface board, the VB-1, from Video Associated Labs in Austin, Texas. Now using the newer VB-3 board, Bernstein praises its capabilities as* "Dynamite. You can knock out the color, blur the effects, superimpose, adjust the color intensity, do all kinds of crazy things. Sometimes, as with the Intelligence Graphics System, I can't record the signal directly for the output, so I just videotape the images with a camera directly off the screen."

Microcomputers present a new medium to the artist. As Bernstein stated in a telephone interview, "There is only one medium that comes close to it and that's a stained glass window." In almost all other uses of color by the artist, the light is reflected off the image. With the microcomputer screen the light is refracted and transmitted to the viewer creating an entirely new means of expression.

Software exists today that can give this new art form to the public. Programs such as *Paint* by Reston Publishing Company (for the Atari 800) gives the user creative control of the screen as a surface. It allows colors, textures, different brush strokes to be selected and freely placed on the screen by game paddle control. There is total freedom to create images, to enlarge them, to "paint" at will.

Programs such as *Paint* offer a wonderful introduction to this new art form. The best part, of course, is that because it is microcomputer based, all people can access and use it.

Of all the tools to come across the educational scene in the last twenty years, the microcomputer is, without question, the most adaptable. Anyone can use it and do so for whatever needs present themselves. It is for this basic reason that the microcomputer will become the common denominator in education.

Future
VII

Whatever the future of microcomputers will bring to society in general, it also will bring to the handicapped.

Before we discuss the long-term effect of microcomputers in education, I would like to share something from the present. Looking toward the future through the eyes of physically handicapped babies may be one of the best ways to understand the full impact of this technology.

At the March 1983 Council for Exceptional Children Conference on Microcomputers in Special Education, held in Hartford, CT, there was a presentation by Mike Behrmann, Ed.D. and Liz Lahm, M.A. from the George Mason University, Fairfax, VA. Their presentation was titled "Critical Learning: Multiple Handicapped Babies Get On-Line." The study group happens to be infants and toddlers, ages birth to thirty months.

To quote from the paper:

> *Severely physically handicapped infants and toddlers are limited in the amount of interaction they can have with their environment. This may limit the amount they can learn from it, causing secondary handicaps and thus creating an even more handicapped individual. This cycle can possibly be broken by using a microcomputer to give some of the environmental interaction back to the infant.*

The paper reveals careful consideration of the research already completed as to how important the early years are for conceptual and language development. That research shows that interaction with one's environment is probably essential to the learning process. It also shows that to assess vicarious learning, it is necessary for interactive behavior to occur on the part of the child.

From the previous research, the stage was set for microcomputer based technology as this further quote from the paper suggests.

Microcomputer based technology is now providing the means to maximize children's ability to interact with their environment (i.e., respond to or initiate an observable action) as well as provide a means to systematically evaluate the consistency and accuracy of those interactions, even though they may be insignificant to the observer. There are three areas in which technology can significantly affect learning by enhancing environmental interactions of the child: communication, environmental control, and environmental manipulation. These three "domains" must be woven together in order to provide teachers and parents with the ability to "teach" these children to function to their fullest potential.

The equipment for the project was described as follows:

The project currently utilizes an Apple II plus microcomputer, Votrx Type 'N Talk voice synthesizer, a color TV monitor, and various custom-made switches as input devices. Efforts are being made to use only readily available commercial hardware to allow for replication of the program at other facilities in the future. The switches, though custom-made, are inexpensive and easy to make or commercially available switches can be substituted.

The eight-level research project was described as follows:

The objectives in level 1 begin with assessing the needs of each individual through an information gathering process. Information related to the optimal working position of the child, the probable best switch and any unique program requirements such as those for visual or hearing impairments are obtained from the teachers, therapists and parents of the child. Using the initial information, objectives at level 2 attempt to establish the cause/effect relationship before requesting the child to learn the concept of decision making. The next levels (3-6) gradually increase the abstractness of the picture representation on the computer screen while teaching the child to make a selection. This is done to allow the child more flexibility and ability in his/her choice vocabulary. These levels also increase the number of pictures or options presented to the child at a given time. The end result will be a system of categorizing choices that will facilitate finding a specific response or choice (levels 7 and 8).

The first three levels of the project (assessment, cause/effect, and concept of choice) have been implemented as a pilot study with ten infants and toddlers. As indicated, this project is ongoing at the time of this writing. At the time of the CEC convention, level 1 and 2 data was under evaluation. Here are the "Implications for Further Research" as stated at that time.

The research design and results thus far represent only the beginning stages of the technology applications research planned. Level 1 and 2 data, when evaluated for approximately eighty children, should provide indicators as to which multi-handicapped children will benefit most from this type of training.

Levels 3-8 of the project will provide a systematic training approach to teach developmentally young children to effectively utilize microcomputer technology to interact with their environment. The technology involved includes use of an Apple II plus, voice synthesizer, environmental control mechanism (BSR x-10 controller) and robotics (Heath Hero-1). These combined technologies will be programmed so that the child will be able to select options from a "menu." The selection of an option will then be translated into an interaction with the child's environment in a preprogrammed format using one or more of these technologies.

When a child reaches level 8, he/she will be able to select from a variety of categories—robot, communications, environmental control. From these categories additional choices will be available (i.e., robot to get x toy or robot get teacher).

The general purpose of the project is to apply commercially available technology that is relatively inexpensive to the learning needs of developmentally young handicapped children. Technology is growing at an almost uncomprehensible pace, but the technology and need are both present now and the wait for "something better" may never end. The robot which is being utilized in the project was not available six months ago. It may well make some of the hardware obsolete almost before the project starts. This robot can "see," "hear," move about, manipulate objects and turn off and on switches. Thus, it may have already removed the necessity of an environmental controller and voice synthesis communication. What has not changed though, is the need to systematically train handicapped individuals to utilize technology that can benefit them.

Systematic training can be done in such a manner that the technology and/or application can change while the "format and interaction mechanism" between the handicapped individual and the technology remains the same. If one thinks of one of the major problems for training severely and profoundly handicapped—training the handicapped person to generalize from one situation to another—the potential is there for developing a constant format for enabling an individual to make choices while others "programming" the technology to generalize or adapt to different environments.

It is hoped that the capabilities of microcomputer systems to extend environmental interactions to infants of limited motor abilities will provide them with the consistent control of their environment necessary for normal concept development. This in turn should affect the language development, self-concept development, ability to communicate and their social interactions. By developing these skills at normal developmental ages it is hoped that secondary handicaps will be prevented. As their skills advance, the technology can advance with them, always giving them appropriate opportunities for interaction and communication. Ultimately, they will have the ability to reach outside their immediate environment by using telecommunication networks. This will enable them to transmit information or communicate with others through telephone and television lines.

The findings of this research should impact other populations of handicapped individuals in addition to the physically handicapped. It can have direct application to all individuals who have a mental age in the range of zero through thirty months, as studied in this project. Mentally handicapped individuals who have additional physical handicaps should also be able to utilize a similar approach regardless of their age.

These babies may never face the full impact of their inability to move freely. Through single switches, they will be able to control, even command the environment around them. They will have the ability to bring parts of the outside world to their side under their control. What this early interaction with the real world will mean to the learning process is staggering. It represents a future without total dependence on others and without isolation. It may give these children some capability to fill their "normal needs," as well as their special requirements.

What will the real future hold for these children? What impact will their ability to control robotic devices have on their environment? How will this new environment affect learning? These are a few of the questions that will start being answered by the research now underway.

Microcomputer usage will have a dramatic effect on all handicapped children in the future of their learning as well as their placement in society. Tomorrow's jobs will all use microcomputers as part of the job description. Knowing how to use this tool will become a standard job requirement in all segments of our society. That is why teaching handicapped children how to use this machine *now* is so important. It will give them a head start, not only for their educational needs of the moment, but for their career placement in the future.

And what of the microcomputer of tomorrow? How will it differ from those available today? Smaller, more portable, perhaps. Common software will probably not be on tape or disks but rather as "firmware" (ROM chips that plug into the central unit) that will give the microcomputer built-in features like word processing and communications. More portability will come with liquid crystal displays. They will replace the more cumbersome TV/monitors. There will be more sophisticated entry systems such as voice entry, making the microcomputer a servant by common speech control. All of these technologies exist today and are making their way into the marketplace. There will be refinements and improvements and, before long, serious price reductions as these technologies leave the testing stage and move into mass production.

Two relatively new technologies, robotics and interactive video disks, will have dramatic effects on education in general but even more profound effects for the handicapped. Both provide major breakthroughs in the use of microcomputers in education.

The robotics of the future could serve the needs of the physically handicapped in very direct ways. Even the first generation robots like HERO-1 from Heath/Zenith Educational Systems are already at work in research projects like that of Behrmann and Lahm.

HERO-1 is twenty inches high and looks much like a relative of R2D2. It can sense sound, motion, light, time and distance. It can move about a room, pick up and deliver objects with its programmable arm and will talk to you with its speech synthesizer. This is today. What of the next generation of HEROs? If the technology grows (and you can be sure it will), what will HERO-2 be capable of doing? It is entirely likely this technology will eventually bring a completely controllable environment to the physically handicapped—from cooking and cleaning to a chess playing companion.

Video disk technology combined with microcomputer technology brings with it the marriage of two very powerful learning tools. The interactive video disk is the result. The interactive capability of the microcomputer combined with the video spectacle of real world images brings together the best recent educational technology has to offer. Dr. Richard Pollak at the Minnesota Educational Computing Consortium (MECC) put it this way, "The video disk alone contains all previous educational technologies rolled into one—from the chalk and slate to the slide/tape show. Combine that with the power of the microcomputer and it's dynamite."

The interactive video of the future will provide specialized training where none could otherwise exist. This will be especially helpful in rural areas or for gifted children, where a teacher may not be available to teach a special subject. It will be used in general education because it can literally bring the real world into the class room through video. And of course what it will mean to the education of the handicapped is, to me at least, its most exciting horizon.

The Real Future

The "information age" is here. There are going to be changes in education. Just when and how those changes will occur is subject to great speculation.

There is an acknowledged need to improve math and science education in elementary and secondary schools. A one billion dollar budget over five years was proposed during 1983 in the U.S. House of Representatives to fund a cure for what some people consider a national crisis. An additional $425 million was proposed for fiscal year 1984 to retrain and recertify teachers in both subjects. Some people say the math-science lag in the United States is a national disaster because it took the perception of a crisis to galvanize the educational system into responding. The ability to recognize future needs of society and to provide the educational curricula that will fill those needs, some say, is lacking in our system of public education. If the math/science lag is used as an example, perhaps there is truth to the statement.

Will the computer revolution that is upon us be another "crisis" condition before it is dealt with by the educational system? I sincerely hope not, but if you look at the number of handicapped children in the system and realize how few have been introduced to the microcomputer, I fear the numbers would serve as another embarrassment to the public education system.

The future education for the handicapped is the responsibility of public education. The implementation of the technology to improve the quality of that education is also their responsibility. If that responsibility is lived up to, the future for the handicapped will certainly be brighter than it is today.

The public education system, by definition, must include parents as well as educators. There must be interest and involvement from the home front. We cannot send the children off to school in the morning and assume that all educational responsibility ends there.

The size and structure of today's educational system has presented problems for many parents. The buildings as well as the curriculum are foreign when compared to the smaller, intimate educational environments of just a few years ago. Some parents are intimidated by the bureaucracy that has somehow insulated them from day-to-day involvement in the education of their children. Some call it parent apathy—parents too busy to care. More likely, it is parent intimidation. As a result, the system has become less responsive to the needs of society. Communication between parents and the system seems to have broken down. By implication this means communication between society and education has diminished. The math/science crisis is a good example of the result.

The advent of the microcomputer age may serve to solve this communication problem. As the dialogue between microcomputers presents itself on the home computer screen, the parent involvement in the educational process will return. A portion of the classroom activities will be in the living room or den, not all in the monolithic structures that have evolved as public schools.

The current fad of predicting the future school as one "without walls" implies the fall of the buildings that have housed the educational system. Is it necessary that the walls crumble to accommodate the future? I don't think so. The pivotal question will undoubtedly be whether the educational system is able to integrate technology into the current structure. This will mean a substantial change in both the teacher role and utilization of the buildings from which education is delivered. But it does not mean that the system must be destroyed to accommodate the change.

There can be a model that provides orderly transition to the microcomputer of today and insures movement with the technology of the future. This model needs to draw heavily from the assets already in place, the manpower as well as the fixed plant. The role of the teacher may develop into that of the true mentor, the stimulus to learning as implied in today's system, but falls short because of the time spent grading papers, keeping records and numerous tasks technology could remove. A machine, no matter how sophisticated, cannot replace the human encounter. The true caring, emotion and feeling necessary for the education of children cannot be built into a machine. This human side of education must always be available and technology may pave the way for more instead of less such interaction.

The buildings will remain the center of interaction as the place to gather for those with common interests and goals. Functionally, a place to sit and take a test is hardly the ultimate use of such space. A place of human experience, guidance, stimulus and leadership development is a far more fitting role for the school building of tomorrow. Here the individual education, the true teaching to the strengths as well as the weaknesses of a child, can be planned and directed, and the delivery system set in motion. The future of the educational system, with such a model, would not only enhance the quality of education but would give back to the educator the rightful role of "teacher" as opposed to clerk in charge of grades.

A Personal Reflection

I look to the world of tomorrow as a place I want to be. In spite of the challenges placed in my path, the tools to meet those challenges can be provided. I want my children's world of tomorrow to be just as attractive. I want them to be able to stand their ground, to experience joy, feel pain and understand that both are a part of living. I want them to have the tools to make their lives meaningful in the society in which they choose to live.

That world of tomorrow will include the computer revolution. My world as well as that of my children will be influenced by that revolution. As a family, we have chosen to join rather than ignore the changes around us. We have found the waters to be inviting, the challenges stimulating and the results rewarding.

As a family, I doubt that we differ from the average. We fight with our kids, the dogs and cats just as much as our neighbors do. If we differ at all, it would be in how we look at technology and how we were motivated and able to integrate it into our lives.

We had a reason, a very strong reason, to get involved with the microcomputer. We had a problem. One of our family members needed help. As we tried to provide that help, we discovered the microcomputer to be a more than suitable tool. As parents of a handicapped child, perhaps we had a stronger motivation to get involved with the microcomputer, but once motivated, the task of actually learning how to use the machine was simple.

Why am I telling you exactly how simple the microcomputer is to use? In order to motivate *you* to try it. Let it help you solve problems. Let it help handicapped children learn and expand their horizons. We also know that if we could do it, so can you. There is nothing difficult about using a microcomputer.

The future of technology for the handicapped rests in the hands of those able to provide the training for its use. The teachers, parents, vocational rehabilitation professionals and medical community all must become aware enough of what *can* be done to be instrumental in seeing that it *is* done. The job at hand is to inform a nation that technology can change the future for the handicapped.

Appendices

The appendices of this book are presented as a quick reference guide to special education implementation of the microcomputer and include both software and hardware reference materials. You will find a directory of educational software producers as well as appendices listing special programs designed for specific disability and interest areas. We have included reference materials, bibliographies and program listings, all with contact information so that you can further investigate the products and information that seem useful to your needs.
    The listings that appear here are not intended to represent all computer products and information that could be useful in special education, but a sampling of some that may be appropriate.
    In many cases price information is also included. However, prices can change without notice, and the information should be viewed as an indication of price range rather than the exact cost of the program.
    All of this bibliographic and appendix information was reprinted with the permission of *Closing The Gap*. The material is part of an on-going data base of information developed for use in *Closing The Gap* and is copyrighted, all rights reserved.

Software Publishers and Distributors

A

The following listing of software publishers and distributors is presented in alphabetical order. The major contact information for catalog ordering is listed, along with a quick reference guide to the educational skill areas in which the companies have published software. In addition the microcomputer brands which each company supports is indicated. It does not include every educational software producer but the list should give you a good start on finding software products in the skill areas and your desired brand of microcomputer.

This is a list of general education software publishers as well as special education producers. It is designed to give you the information you will need to contact producers directly.

How To Use This Directory

Each producer or distributor is listed with name, address, city, state, zip code and telephone number. In addition the microcomputer brands supported by the individual publisher are listed. Following each company are a string of Xs in the appropriate boxes representing the academic skill areas of software production. If you are looking for Language Arts programs for the Apple, check the companies with Xs in the second column (*Language Arts*) and refer to the last line of each listing for the Apple software producers. Using this method will give you a comprehensive list of companies publishing material in the skill areas you are interested in for your brand of microcomputer.

	Math	Language Arts	Reading	Spelling	Science	Social Studies	Geography	Basic Living Skills	Music	Art	Games	Foreign Languages	Library Skills	Prereading	Physical Education	Authoring Systems	Word Processing	Typing Tutor	Business Education	Computer Literacy	Miscellaneous	Administration	Special Needs
APX (Atari Program Exchange) P.O. Box 3705 Santa Clara, CA 95055 (800) 538-1862 Atari	x	x	x	x	x	x	x	x	x	x	x	x	x	x	x	x	x	x	x	x			x
Abbott Educational Software 334 Westwood Avenue East Longmeadow, MA 01028 (413) 525-3462 PET-64		x	x																				
Academic Software 22 E. Quackenbuch Avenue Dumont, NJ 07628 (201) 385-2395 Apple, TRS-80, PET, Vic, Atari	x	x	x	x	x	x	x	x	x	x	x	x	x		x	x	x	x	x	x	x		
Activity Resources Company, Inc. P.O. Box 4875 Hayward, CA 94540 (415) 782-1300 TRS-80, Apple, PET	x																						
Addison-Wesley Publishing Co. Reading, MA 01867 (617) 944-3700 Apple, IBM, TRS-80-III																			x		x		

Ahead Designs
699 N. Vulcan, #88
Encinitas, CA 92024
(619) 436-4071
Apple

American Micro Media.
P.O. Box 306
Red Hook, NY 12571
(914) 756-2557
Apple, Pet, TRS-80

Apple Computer, Inc.
10260 Bandley Drive
Cupertino, CA 95014
(408) 996-1010
Apple

Applied Educational Systems
RFD 2, Box 213
Dunbarton, NH 03301
(603) 774-6151
Apple, Pet, TRS-80

Applied MicroSystems
P.O. Box 832
Roswell, GA 30077
(404) 371-0832
Apple, IBM

Aquarius Publishers, Inc.
P.O. Box 128
Indian Rocks Beach, FL 33535
(813) 595-7890
Apple, TRS-80

Artra Inc.
P.O. Box 653
Arlington, VA 22216
(703) 527-0455
Heath/Zenith H-89

101

	Math	Language Arts	Reading	Spelling	Science	Social Studies	Geography	Basic Living Skills	Music	Art	Games	Foreign Languages	Library Skills	Prereading	Physical Education	Authoring Systems	Word Processing	Typing Tutor	Business Education	Computer Literacy	Miscellaneous	Administration	Special Needs
Atari Home Computer Division	x			x		x	x	x	x	x	x	x	x	x	x	x	x			x			
Athroid Digital, Inc.	x	x	x	x								x					x	x		x			
Avant-Garde Creations		x	x	x	x	x	x				x	x				x				x		x	x
Banana, Inc.	x	x	x	x	x	x	x	x	x	x	x	x	x	x	x	x	x	x	x	x	x	x	x
Bank Street College of Education																x							

Atari Home Computer Division
P.O. Box 50047
San Jose, CA 95150
(800) 538-8543
Atari

Athroid Digital, Inc.
P.O. Box 1385
Tittsfield, MA 01202
(413) 448-8278
Apple

Avant-Garde Creations
P.O. Box 30160
Eugene, OR 97403
(503) 345-3043
Apple, IBM, Atari

Banana, Inc.
P.O. Box 2868, 3400 Executive Pky.
Toledo, OH 43606
(419) 531-7100
Apple, Atari, IBM

Bank Street College of Education
610 West 112th St.
New York, NY 10025
(212) 663-7200
Apple, Atari, Commodore 64

			x									x	x
	x		x		x							x	
	x		x									x	
	x												
	x							x					
			x								x		
			x										
	x		x			x					x		
	x												
	x												
	x			x							x		
	x	x			x								
	x	x			x						x		
	x	x	x		x								
	x	x	x	x	x								
x										x			

Basics and Beyond, Inc.
P.O. Box 10, Pinesbridge Road
Amawalk, NY 10501
(914) 962-2355
Atari, TRS-80 I & II

Bell & Howell Microcomputer
7100 N. McCormick Road
Chicago, IL 60645
(312) 673-3300
Apple

Borg-Warner Educational Systems
600 W. University Dr.
Arlington Heights, IL 60004
(800) 323-7577
Apple, TRS-80

BrainBank, Inc.
Suite 408, 220 Fifth Avenue
New York, NY 10001
(212) 686-6565
Apple, TRS-80, PET

Broderbund Software
1938 4th Street
San Rafael, CA 94901
(415) 456-6424
Apple, Atari

COMP.O.S.E.
6500 W. 95th St.
Oak Lawn, IL 60453
(312) 599-5550
Apple

COMPress
P.O. Box 102
Wentworth, NH 03282
(603) 764-5831
Apple

103

	Math	Language Arts	Reading	Spelling	Science	Social Studies	Geography	Basic Living Skills	Music	Art	Games	Foreign Languages	Library Skills	Prereading	Physical Education	Authoring Systems	Word Processing	Typing Tutor	Business Education	Computer Literacy	Miscellaneous	Administration	Special Needs
California School for the Deaf 39350 Gallaudet Dr. Fremont, CA 94538 (415) 794-3666 Apple															x					x		x	
Charles Mann and Associates 7594 San Remo Trail Yucca Valley, CA 92284 (619) 365-9718 Apple, IBM																			x		x		
Comaldor P.O. Box 356, Postal Station O Toronto, Ontario Canada M4A2N9 (416) 751-7481 PET	x		x	x	x	x	x		x		x		x								x	x	
Comm Data Computer House, Inc. P.O. Box 325 Milford, MI 48042 (313) 685-0113 Commodore	x	x		x																			
Compu-Tations, Inc. P.O. Box 502 Troy, MI 48099 (313) 689-5059 Apple II, Atari 800	x	x		x							x	x		x	x		x			x		x	

Compumax, Inc.
P.O. Box 7239
Menlo Park, CA 94025
(415) 854-6700
Atari

Computer Advanced Ideas, Inc.
1442A Walnut Street, Suite 3 1
Berkeley, CA 94709
(415) 526-9100
Apple, IBM

Computer Software/Books R US
16 Birdsong
Irvine, CA 92714
(714) 559-5120
Apple, Atari, Pet, TRS-80, IBM, CP/M

Computer Station
11610 Page Service Dr.
St. Louis MO 63141
(314) 432-7019
Apple

Computers to Help People, Inc.
1221 West Johnson Street
Madison, WI 53715
(608) 257-5917
Apple II Plus

Concept Educational Software
P.O. Box 6184
Allentown, PA 18001
(215) 266-1679
TRS-80 Mod I or II

Conduit
100 Lindquist Center
Univ. of Iowa
P.O. Box 388
Iowa City, IA 52244
(319) 353-5789
Apple, TRS-80, Atari, PET

	Math	Language Arts	Reading	Spelling	Science	Social Studies	Geography	Basic Living Skills	Music	Art	Games	Foreign Languages	Library Skills	Prereading	Physical Education	Authoring Systems	Word Processing	Typing Tutor	Business Education	Computer Literacy	Miscellaneous	Administration	Special Needs
Control Data Publishing Co. P.O. Box 261127 San Diego, CA 92126 (800) 233-3784 Apple, Atari, Texas Instruments	x											x											
Convergent Systems Inc. 245 E 6th St. St. Paul, MN 55101 (612) 221-0587 TI, Apple	x	x	x	x							x	x								x			
Cow Bay Computing P.O. Box 515 Manhasset, NY 11020 (516) 365-4423 PET, Comm-64	x			x	x		x				x									x	x		
Cross Educational Software P.O. Box 1536 Ruston, LA 71279 (318) 255-8921 Apple				x	x								x		x	x				x	x		
Data Command P.O. Box 548 Kankakee, IL 60901 (815) 933-7735 Apple, TRS-80 I & III	x	x	x								x												

Publisher												
Developmental Learning Materials One DLM Park Allen, TX 75002 (214) 248-6300 Apple IIe, TI-99/4A		x		x		x					x	x
Dormac, Inc. 8034 S.W. Nimbus Beaverton, OR 97005 (800) 547-8032 Apple		x					x					
Duxbury Systems, Inc. 77 Great Road Acton, MA 07120 (617) 263-7761 CP/M						x	x					
Dynacomp, Inc. 1427 Monroe Avenue Rochester, NY 14618 (716) 442-8960 Apple, Atari, IBM, TRS I&III, PET-64		x				x	x x			x		
Joseph Nichols Publisher P.O. Box 2394 Tulsa, OK 74101 (918) 583-3390 TRS-80 Model III				x								
Project C.A.I.S.H., Gocio Ele. Sch. 3450 Gocio Road Sarasota, FL 33580 (813) 355-3567 Apple II									x			
Project REACT 66 Malcolm Ave. SE Minneapolis, MN 55414 (612) 379-0428 Apple II											x	x

Vendor	Math	Language Arts	Reading	Spelling	Science	Social Studies	Geography	Basic Living Skills	Music	Art	Games	Foreign Languages	Library Skills	Prereading	Physical Education	Authoring Systems	Word Processing	Typing Tutor	Business Education	Computer Literacy	Miscellaneous	Administration	Special Needs
Carl Geigner, 1603 Court Street, Syracuse, NY 13208; Apple II																							x
EDIS Systems, Inc., 422 Main St., Lafayette, IN 47901, (317) 742-1787; Apple II, TRS-80, Mod III																							
EISI, 2225 Grant Road, Suite 3, Los Altos, CA 94022, (415) 969-5212; Apple, Atari, TRS-80, TI, PET	x	x	x	x	x	x	x				x	x				x	x	x	x	x	x		
EX-ED Computer Systems, Inc., 71-11 112th St., Forest Hills, NY 11375, (212) 268-0020; any running CP/M				x																	x		
Early Games Educational Software, Shelard Plaza North, Suite 140C, Minneapolis, MN 55426, (612) 544-4720; Apple II, Atari, IBM, TRS-80 Mod III & CC	x									x	x		x								x		

108

		x	x				x		x	
			x		x		x			
			x		x		x			
				x			x		x	
							x			
			x		x		x		x	
							x			
					x		x			
	x		x	x	x	x	x		x	
							x			
							x			
							x			
							x			
	x			x	x	x	x			
					x		x			
			x				x	x		
		x	x	x		x	x	x		

Earthware Computer Services
Box 30039
Eugene, OR 97403
(503) 344-3383
Apple

Edu-Comp, Inc.
14109 S. E. 168th St.
Renton, WA 98055
(206) 255-7410
Apple

Edu-Soft
4639 Spruce St.
Philadelphia, PA 19139
(215) 747-1284
Apple II, Atari, TRS-80

Edu-Ware Services
28035 Dorothy Drive
Agoura, CA 91301
(213) 706-0661
Apple, Atari, IBM

EduTech
634 Commonwealth Ave.
Newton Centre, MA 02159
(617) 965-4813
Apple

Educational Activities, Inc.
P.O. Box 392
Freeport, NY 11520
(800) 645-3739
Apple, PET TRS-80, Atari

Educational Computing
Systems, Inc.
136 Fairbanks Road
Oakridge, TN 37830
(615) 483-4915
Apple II

	Math	Language Arts	Reading	Spelling	Science	Social Studies	Geography	Basic Living Skills	Music	Art	Games	Foreign Languages	Library Skills	Prereading	Physical Education	Authoring Systems	Word Processing	Typing Tutor	Business Education	Computer Literacy	Miscellaneous	Administration	Special Needs
Educational Micro Systems, Inc. P.O. Box 471 Chester, NJ 07930 (201) 879-5982 TRS-80 I & III, Apple	x																					x	
Educational Software Midwest 414 Rosemere Lane Maquoketa, IA 52060 (319) 652-2334 Apple																					x		
Educational Software and Marketing 1035 Outerpark Drive Springfield, IL 62704 (217) 787-4594 Apple, TRS-80 III	x		x						x	x	x	x	x			x			x		x		
Educational Software, Inc. 4565 Cherryvale Soquel, CA 95073 (408) 476-4901 Atari, Comm-64, Vic										x													
Educational Systems Software P.O. Box E El Toro, CA 92630 (714) 768-2916 Apple																				x	x		

Company										
Educational Teaching Aids 159 W. Kinzie Chicago, IL 60610 (312) 644-9438 Apple, Commodore, TRS-80	x	x					x			
Educulture 1 Dubuque Plaza, Suite 803 Dubuque, IA 52001 (800) 553-4858 Apple		x								
Edupro P.O. Box 51346 Palo Alto, CA 94303 (415) 494-2790 Atari	x			x					x	
Eiconics, Inc. P.O. Box 1207, 211 Cruz Alta Rd. Taos, NM 87571 (505) 758-1696 Apple					x					
Electronic Courseware Systems P.O. Box 2374, Station A Champaign, IL 60820 (217) 359-7099 Apple	x						x	x	x	
Elwyn Institutes 111 Elwyn Road Elwyn, PA 19063 (215) 358-6400 TRS-80 Mod. III										
Encyclopedia Britannica Ed. Corp. 425 N. Michigan Ave. Chicago, IL 60611 (800) 554-9862								x	x	x

111

Company	Math	Language Arts	Reading	Spelling	Science	Social Studies	Geography	Basic Living Skills	Music	Art	Games	Foreign Languages	Library Skills	Prereading	Physical Education	Authoring Systems	Word Processing	Typing Tutor	Business Education	Computer Literacy	Miscellaneous	Administration	Special Needs
Entelek P.O. Box 1303 Portsmouth, NH 03801 (603) 436-0439 Apple	x																						
Evans Newton Inc. 7745 E. Redfield Road, Suite 100 Scottsdale, AZ 85160 (602) 998-2777 Apple, PET, TRS-80																					x		
Financial Analysis Service P.O. Box 1937 Hiram, Ohio 44234 (216) 569-3201 Apple															x						x		
Fireside Computing, Inc. 5843 Montgomery Road Elkridge, MD 21227 (301) 796-4165 TRS-80 I or III	x	x	x	x	x	x				x	x	x	x		x	x	x	x	x	x			
Follett Library Book Co. 4506 Northeast Highway Crystal Lake, IL 60014 (800) 435-6170 Apple, Atari, Comm., TRS-80																							

Fullmer Assoc.
1132 Via Jose
San Jose, CA 95120
(408) 997–1154
Apple

Funk Vocab-Ware
4825 Province Line Road
Princeton, NJ 08540
(609) 921–0245
Apple II

GRAFex Company
P.O. Box 1558
Cupertino, CA 95015
(408) 996–2689
Atari

George Earl Software
1320 South Gen. McMullan
San Antonio, TX 78237
(512) 434–3681
Apple, TRS-80

Gladstone Electronics
901 Fuhrmann Blvd.
Buffalo, NY 14203
(716) 849–0735
Timex Sinclair

Green Valley Informantics
769 N. Sacre Lane
Monmouth, OR 97361
(503) 838–1172
PET, CBM

Grover and Associates
7 Mt. Lassen Dr. D116
San Rafael, CA 94903
(415) 479–5906
Apple II or II Plus

	Math	Language Arts	Reading	Spelling	Science	Social Studies	Geography	Basic Living Skills	Music	Art	Games	Foreign Languages	Library Skills	Prereading	Physical Education	Authoring Systems	Word Processing	Typing Tutor	Business Education	Computer Literacy	Miscellaneous	Administration	Special Needs
Harcourt Brace Javanovich	x																				x		
Harper & Row	x	x	x	x	x	x												x				x	
Hartley Courseware, Inc.	x	x	x	x	x	x					x		x	x	x					x	x	x	
Hayden Book Company, Inc.	x	x	x													x	x		x				
Holt, Rinehart, and Winston																					x		

Harcourt Brace Javanovich
1250 6th Avenue
San Diego, CA 92101
(800) 543-1918
Apple, TRS-80, Atari

Harper & Row
10 East 53rd Street
New York, NY 10022
(212) 593-7000
Apple

Hartley Courseware, Inc.
P.O. Box 431
Dimondale, MI 48821
(616) 942-8987
Apple

Hayden Book Company, Inc.
600 Sussolk
Lowell, MS 01853
(800) 343-1218
Apple, Atari, PET

Holt, Rinehart, and Winston
383 Madison Ave.
New York, NY 10017
(212) 872-2000
Apple, PET, TRS-80

	x											
					x						x	
						x					x	
					x						x	x
					x	x					x	x
					x	x					x	x
											x	
		x				x				x		
						x					x	
		x		x		x		x		x		
										x		
					x					x		
										x		
					x					x		
		x	x	x			x			x	x	
		x					x			x	x	
		x		x		x		x		x	x	
				x			x		x	x	x	
	x			x						x	x	

I.O.R. Enterprises
Rt. 6, Box 20
Chapel Hill, NC 27514
(919) 929-4825
Apple II Plus

Ideatech Company
P.O. Box 62451
Sunnyvale, CA 94088
(408) 985-7591
Apple

Information Unlimited Software
281 Arlington Avenue
Berkeley, CA 94707
(415) 331-6700
Apple, IBM, TI

Instant Software
Peterborough, NH 03458
(800) 343-0728
Apple, TRS-80, TI, PET

Instructional/Comm Tech Inc.
10 Stepar Place,
Huntington Station, NY 11746
(516) 549-3000
Apple

J & S Software, Inc.
140 Reid Avenue
Port Washington, NY 11050
(516) 944-9304
Apple, TRS-80 I & III

J. L. Hammett
Box 545
Braintree, MA 02184
(800) 225-5467
Apple, Atari, IBM, PET, TRS-80

Company	Math	Language Arts	Reading	Spelling	Science	Social Studies	Geography	Basic Living Skills	Music	Art	Games	Foreign Languages	Library Skills	Prereading	Physical Education	Authoring Systems	Word Processing	Typing Tutor	Business Education	Computer Literacy	Miscellaneous	Administration	Special Needs
JMH Software	x	x	x	x	x			x			x		x							x	x		
Jagdstaffel Software		x																					
Jamestown Publishers		x																					
K-12 Micromedia	x	x	x	x	x	x	x	x	x	x	x	x	x	x	x	x	x	x	x	x	x		
Krell Software Corporation	x	x	x	x	x	x			x		x		x							x			
Apple, Atari, TRS-80 I & III, Com. PET & 64	x																			x		x	

JMH Software
4850 Wellington Lane
Minneapolis, MN 55442
(612) 559-4790
Atari, Commodore PET, Vic, 64

Jagdstaffel Software
608 Blossom Hill Road
San Jose, CA 95123
(408) 578-1643
Apple

Jamestown Publishers
P.O. Box 6743
Providence, RI 02940
(401) 351-1915
Apple II & IIe

K-12 Micromedia
P.O. Box 17
Valley Cottage, NY 10989
(201) 391-7555
Apple, Atari, TRS-80 I & III, PET

Krell Software Corporation
1320 Stony Brook Rd
Stony Brook, NY 11790
(516) 751-5139
Apple, Atari, TRS-80 I & III, Com.
PET & 64

	x			x						
				x			x		x	x
					x			x		
				x	x					
					x					
					x					
					x		x			
	x	x		x	x			x		
						x				

Bruce Land & David Farmer
395 Brooktondale Road
Brooktondale, NY 14817
Apple II

Lara Software
980 Hunting Valley Place
Decatur, GA 30033
(404) 634-7601
Apple

Laureate Learning Systems, Inc.
1 Mill Street
Burlington, VT 05401
(802) 862-7355
Apple II

Learning Company
4370 Alpine Road
Portola Valley, CA 94025
(415) 851-3160
Apple, Atari, TRS color

Learning Systems
P.O. Box 15
Marblehead, MA 01945
(617) 639-0114
Apple II, DEC, IBM, TRS-80

Learning Systems, Ltd.
P.O. Box 9046
Fort Collins, CO 80525
(303) 482-6193

Learning Tools
686 Massachusetts Ave.
Cambridge, MA 02139
(617) 864-8086
Apple II & III, IBM, DEC

117

Category	Learning Tree Software	Learning Well	Lightning Software	Love Publishing	MARAC
Math	x	x			x
Language Arts		x			x
Reading	x	x			x
Spelling					x
Science					x
Social Studies					x
Geography					x
Basic Living Skills					x
Music					x
Art					
Games	x	x			x
Foreign Languages					
Library Skills					x
Prereading	x	x			x
Physical Education				x	x
Authoring Systems					x
Word Processing			x		x
Typing Tutor					x
Business Education					x
Computer Literacy					x
Miscellaneous				x	x
Administration				x	x
Special Needs					

Learning Tree Software, Inc.
Box 246
Kings Park, NY 11754
(516) 462-6216
Pet, Commodore 64

Learning Well
200 South Service Road
Roslyn Heights, NY 11577
(516) 621-1540
Apple II

Lightning Software
P.O. Box 5223
Stanford, CA 94305
(415) 327-3280
Apple, Atari, IBM-PC

Love Publishing
1777 South Bellaire St.
Denver, CO 80222
(303) 757-2579
Apple II

MARAC
280 Linden Avenue
Branford, CT 06405
(203) 481-3271
Apple, Atari, TRS-80, Comm.

MCE, Inc.
157 S. Kalamazoo Mall
Kalamazoo, MI 49007
(616) 345-8681
Apple II, IIe

MEAN (Ed. Turnkey Systems)
256 North Washington St.
Falls Church, Virginia 22046
(703) 536-2310
Apple, IBM, TI

MECC (Minn. Ed. Comp. Consortium)
2520 Broadway Drive
St. Paul, MN 55113
(612) 638-0627
Apple, Atari

MIND
50 Washington Street
Norwalk, CT 06854
(203) 846-3435
Apple II, TRS-80

MUSE (Micro Users Software Exchange)
347 Charles St.
Baltimore, MD 21201
(301) 659-7212
Apple, Atari

Mathware
919 14th Street
Hermosa Beach, CA 90254
(213) 379-1570
Apple II

McGraw-Hill Gregg Division
1221 Avenue of the Americas
New York, NY 10020
(800) 223-4180
Apple, TRS-80

	Math	Language Arts	Reading	Spelling	Science	Social Studies	Geography	Basic Living Skills	Music	Art	Games	Foreign Languages	Library Skills	Prereading	Physical Education	Authoring Systems	Word Processing	Typing Tutor	Business Education	Computer Literacy	Miscellaneous	Administration	Special Needs
McKiligan Supply Corp. Dist. 435 Main St. Johnson City, NY 13790 (607) 729-6511 Apple, TI, Atari, IBM, Comm	x	x	x	x	x	x	x	x	x	x	x	x	x	x	x	x	x	x	x		x		
Media Materials, Inc. 2936 Remington Ave. Baltimore, MD 21211 (301) 235-1700 Apple, TRS-80 III	x	x																					
Merit Micro Software Corporation 404 Texas Commerce Bank Bldg. Amarillo, TX 79101 (806) 353-7888	x				x															x			
Merlan Scientific Ltd. 247 Armstrong Avenue Georgetown, Ontario Canada L7G 4X6 (416) 877-0171 Apple, PET		x		x				x	x		x		x									x	
Merry Bee Communications 815 Crest Drive Omaha, NE 68046 (402) 592-3479 Apple																							

Company												
Metrologic Publications 143 Harding Avenue Bellmawr, NJ 08031 (609) 933-0100 Apple, TRS-80, PET	x											x
Micro Computer Service, Inc. 2885 East Aurora Ave., Suite 14B Boulder, CO 80303 (303) 447-9471 CP/M					x							x
Micro Lab Learning Center 2310 Skokie Valley Road Highland Park, IL 60035 (312) 433-7550 Apple, IBM	x					x			x	x		
Micro Learningware P.O. Box 307 Mankato, MN 56001 (507) 625-2205 Apple, TRS-80 III, PET	x	x	x	x	x	x	x		x		x	x
Micro Power & Light Company 12820 Hillcrest Road, Suite 224 Dallas, TX 75230 (214) 239-6620 Apple	x	x	x	x	x	x				x	x	
Micro-Ed, Inc. P.O. Box 24156 Minneapolis, MN 55424 (612) 926-2292 Apple, TI, Comm	x	x	x	x				x			x	
MicroGnome (Div. of Fireside) 5843 Montgomery Rd. Elkridge, MD 21227 (301) 796-4165 TRS-80, CPM									x	x	x	

Supplier	Math	Language Arts	Reading	Spelling	Science	Social Studies	Geography	Basic Living Skills	Music	Art	Games	Foreign Languages	Library Skills	Prereading	Physical Education	Authoring Systems	Word Processing	Typing Tutor	Business Education	Computer Literacy	Miscellaneous	Administration	Special Needs
Microcomputer Workshops	x	x			x							x											
Microcomputers Corporation																				x			
Micrograms, Inc.																			x	x			
Micromatics, Inc.	x	x		x	x																x	x	
Microphys Programs	x	x		x	x						x										x	x	

Microcomputer Workshops
103 Puritan Drive
Port Chester, NY 10573
(914) 937-5440
Apple, Atari, TRS-80, PET, Comm 64

Microcomputers Corporation
P.O. Box 8
Armonk, NY 10504
(914) 273-6480
Texas Instruments

Micrograms, Inc.
P.O. Box 2146
Loves Park, IL 61130
(815) 965-2464
Pet, Vic

Micromatics, Inc.
181 No. 200 West, Suite 5
Bountiful, UT 84010
(801) 292-2458
Apple, TRS-80

Microphys Programs
2048 Ford Street
Brooklyn, NY 11229
(212) 646-0140
Apple, TRS-80, PET, Comm 64

	x		x		x			x		x
			x							
									x	
									x	
						x				
				x						
						x				
					x					
					x		x			
					x	x				

Microsoft Services
P.O. Box 776
Harrisonburg, VA 22801
(703) 433-9485
TRS-80 III

Microsoftware Services
P.O. Box 776
Harrisonburg, VA 22801
(703) 433-9485
TRS-80 III

Midwest Software
Box 214
Farmington, MI 48024
(313) 477-0897
Apple, Pet

Milliken Publishing Company
1100 Research Blvd.
St. Louis, MO 63132
(314) 991-4220
Apple, Atari

Milton Bradley
443 Shaker Road
East Longmeadow, MA 01028
(413) 525-6411
Apple, TI

Mount Castor Industries
368 Shays Street
Amherst, MA 01002
(413) 253-3634
Apple, TRS-80, Comm.

Msss D, Inc.
3412 Binkley
Dallas, TX 75205
(214) 522-8051
Apple

123

	Math	Language Arts	Reading	Spelling	Science	Social Studies	Geography	Basic Living Skills	Music	Art	Games	Foreign Languages	Library Skills	Prereading	Physical Education	Authoring Systems	Word Processing	Typing Tutor	Business Education	Computer Literacy	Miscellaneous	Administration	Special Needs
Musitronic P.O. Box 441, 555 Park Drive Owatonna, MN 55060 (507) 451-7871 Apple									x														
N.I.R.E., Don Selwyn 97 Decker Road Butler, NJ 07405 (201) 838-2500 TRS-80 I & III	x																						
Nova Software P.O. Box 545 Alexandria, MN 56308 (612) 762-8016 Apple II													x			x							x
Opportunities For Learning, Inc. 8950 Lurline Avenue. Dept. 26C Chatsworth, CA 91311 (213) 341-2535 Apple, TRS-80, Atari, PET	x	x	x		x	x	x	x	x	x	x	x						x	x			x	
Orange Cherry Media 7 Delano Drive Bedford Hills, NY 10507 (914) 666-8434 Apple, Atari, PET, TRS-80	x	x	x	x	x	x	x				x		x										

PIE, Inc
1714 Illinois St.
Lawrence, KS 66044
(913) 841-3095
Apple

Personal Software Inc. (Visicorp)
2895 Zanker Road
San Jose, CA 95134
(408) 946-9000
Apple, IBM

Potomac MicroResources, Inc.
P.O. Box 277
Riverdale, MD 20737
(301) 864-4444
Apple II

Powell Associates, Inc.
3724 Jefferson, Suite 205
Austin, TX 78731
(800) 531-5239
Apple CP/M, TRS-80 II & III

Powersoft
P.O. Box 157
Pitman, NJ 08071
(609) 589-5500
Apple

PracEd Tapes, Inc.
12162 SE 14th St.
Bellevue, WA 98005
(206) 747-8485
Commodore

Precision People, Inc.
P.O. Box 17402
Jacksonville, FL 32216
(904) 642-1980
TRS-80 I & III

	Math	Language Arts	Reading	Spelling	Science	Social Studies	Geography	Basic Living Skills	Music	Art	Games	Foreign Languages	Library Skills	Prereading	Physical Education	Authoring Systems	Word Processing	Typing Tutor	Business Education	Computer Literacy	Miscellaneous	Administration	Special Needs
Problem Solving Through Strategy Oliva Public School Oliva, MN 56377 (612) 523-1031 Apple											x												
Program Design, Inc. 11 Idar Court Greenwich, CT 06830 (203) 661-8799																							
Programs For Learning, Inc. P.O. Box 954 New Milford, CT 06776 (203) 355-3452 Apple, TRS-80, PET					x																		
G. Evan Rushakoff New Mexico State University Las Cruces, NM 88003 (505) 646-2801 Apple II																							x
Prentke Romich Company 8769 Township Road 513 Shreve, OH 44676 (216) 567-2906 Apple II																	x						x

126

Program Design, Inc.
11 Idar Court
Greenwich, CT 06830
(203) 661-8799
Apple II, Atari

Quality Educational Designs
P.O. Box 12486
Portland, OR 97212
(503) 287-8137
Apple, TRS-80, PET, Comm 64

Queue, Inc.
5 Chapel Hill Drive
Fairfield, CT 06432
(800) 232-2224
Apple, Atari, Comm, TRS-80

Radio Shack (Education Division)
1600 Tandy Center
Fort Worth, TX 76102
(817) 390-3302
TRS-80 all models

Raised Dot Computing
310 S 7th Street
Lewisburg, PA 17837
(717) 523-6739
Apple

Random House School Division
400 Hahn Road
Westminster, MD 21157
(800) 638-6460
Apple, TRS-80

Readers Digest
Pleasantville, NY 10570
(914) 769-7000
Apple, Atari, TRS-80

Math	Language Arts	Reading	Spelling	Science	Social Studies	Geography	Basic Living Skills	Music	Art	Games	Foreign Languages	Library Skills	Prereading	Physical Education	Authoring Systems	Word Processing	Typing Tutor	Business Education	Computer Literacy	Miscellaneous	Administration	Special Needs
x			x							x				x		x						
x									x	x					x				x			
															x						x	
											x											
x	x																					
x	x																					

Quality Educational Software
P.O. Box 502
Troy, MI 48099
(313) 689-5059
Apple, Atari

Reston Publishing Co., Inc.
11480 Sunset Hills Road
Reston, VA 22090
(800) 336-0338
Apple, Atari

Robert E. Stepp III
Station A, P.O. Box 5002
Champaign, IL 61820
(217) 359-7933
Apple II

Rocky Mountain Software, Inc.
214-131 Water Street
Vancouver, B.C.
Canada V6B 4M3
Apple II

SEI (Sliwa Enterprises, Inc.)
P.O. Box 7266, 2013
Cunningham Dr.
Hampton, VA 23666
(804) 826-3777
Apple

					x		x						
				x				x		x			
									x	x			
				x					x				
				x									
				x		x							
		x											
								x					
				x		x	x						
				x			x						
				x									
				x		x							
	x			x		x	x	x					
				x		x	x						
			x		x	x							

SLED Software
P.O. Box 16322
Minneapolis, MN 55416
(612) 926-5820
PET

San Juan Unified School Dist.
6141 Sutter Ave.
Carmichael, CA 95608
(916) 944-3614
Apple

Scholastic Software
904 Sylvan Avenue
Englewood Cliffs, NJ 07632
(212) 944-7700
Apple, Atari, PET, TRS-80, TI

School & Home Courseware, Inc.
1341 Bulldog Lane, Suite C
Fresno, CA 93710
(209) 227-4341
Apple II

Science Research Associates, Inc.
155 North Wacker Drive
Chicago, IL 60606
(800) 621-0664
Apple, Atari, TI

Scott, Foresman Elec. Publishing
1900 East Lake Avenue
Glenview, IL 60025
(312) 729-3000
Apple, Atari, TI

Sensible Software
6619 Derham Drive
West Blomfield, MI 48033
(313) 399-8877
Apple

	Math	Language Arts	Reading	Spelling	Science	Social Studies	Geography	Basic Living Skills	Music	Art	Games	Foreign Languages	Library Skills	Prereading	Physical Education	Authoring Systems	Word Processing	Typing Tutor	Business Education	Computer Literacy	Miscellaneous	Administration	Special Needs
Serendipity Systems, Inc.																			x			x	
Sierra On Line		x	x								x		x										
Skillcorp Software																x	x						
Sof/Sys, Inc.		x																					
Softswap	x	x	x	x	x	x	x	x	x	x	x					x				x			

Serendipity Systems, Inc.
419 W. Seneca St.
Ithaca, NY 14850
(607) 277-4889
Apple

Sierra On Line
36575 Mudge Ranch Road
Coarsegold, CA 93614
(209) 683-6858
Apple

Skillcorp Software
1711 McGaw Ave.
Irvine, CA 92714
(800) 845-8688
Apple, PET, TRS-80

Sof/Sys, Inc.
4306 Upyon Ave. So.
Minneapolis, MN 55410
(612) 929-7104
Apple II, IBM

Softswap
333 Main St.
Redwood City, CA 94063
(415) 363-5470
Apple, public domain programs

Software Connections, Inc.
1800 Wyatt Drive, Suite #17
Santa Clara, CA 95054
(408) 988-3704
Apple

Software Research
P.O. Box 1700
Victoria, BC
Canada VFW 2Y2
(604) 477-7246
Apple, IBM

Software Technology, Inc.
3763 Airport Road
Mobile, AL 36608
(205) 344-7600
Apple, IBM, CP/M

SouthWest EdPsych Services
P.O. Box 1870
Phoenix, AZ 85001
(602) 253-6528
Apple

Southeastern Educational
Software
3300 Buckeye Road
Atlanta, GA 30341
(404) 457-8336
Apple

Southern Microsystems For Ed.
P.O. Box 1981
Burlington, NC 27215
(919) 226-7610
Apple II & III, TRS-80 3, IBM

Spinnaker Software
215 First Street
Cambridge, MA 02142
(617) 868-4700
Apple

Publisher	Math	Language Arts	Reading	Spelling	Science	Social Studies	Geography	Basic Living Skills	Music	Art	Games	Foreign Languages	Library Skills	Prereading	Physical Education	Authoring Systems	Word Processing	Typing Tutor	Business Education	Computer Literacy	Miscellaneous	Administration	Special Needs
Sterling Swift Publishing Co. 1600 Fortview Rd. Austin, TX 78704 (512) 444-7570 Apple	x				x	x						x			x	x			x				x
Stoneware 50 Belvedere San Rafael, CA 94901 (415) 454-6500 Apple																						x	
Strategic Simulations Inc. 883 Stierlin Road, Bldg. A-200 Mountain View, CA 94043 (415) 964-1353 Apple, Atari, TRS-80, IBM						x					x												
SubLOGIC Communications Corp. 713 Edgebrook Drive Champaign, IL 61820 (217) 359-8482 Apple, Atari, TRS-80, IBM		x	x	x		x					x												
Sunburst Communications P.O. Box 40, 39 Washington Ave. Pleasantville, NY 10570 (914) 431-1934 Apple, Atari, TRS-80	x	x	x		x	x								x					x	x			

				x						
	x			x		x			x	
										x
				x						
				x				x		x
		x								
						x	x			
						x	x			
						x				
						x				
			x			x			x	
						x				x
			x			x				
		x	x		x	x	x			
			x	x		x		x		

Sysdata International, Inc.
7671 Old Central Ave., NE
Minneapolis, MN 55432
(612) 780-1750
Apple II

T.H.E.S.I.S.
P.O. Box 147
Garden City, MI 48135
(313) 595-4722
Apple, Atari

TIES
1925 W. County Rd. B2
St. Paul, MN 55113
(612) 633-9100
Apple, Atari

TYC Software
2128 West Jefferson Road
Pittsford, NY 14534
(716) 424-5453
Apple, TRS-80

TYCOM Associates
68 Valma Avenue
Pittsfield, MA 01201
(413) 442-9771
PET

Tamarack Software
P.O. Box 247
Darby, MT 59829
(406) 821-4596
Apple, Atari, PET

Teach Yourself By Computer
Software
2128 W. Jefferson Road
Pittsford, NY 14534
(716) 424-5453
Apple, TRS-80

	Math	Language Arts	Reading	Spelling	Science	Social Studies	Geography	Basic Living Skills	Music	Art	Games	Foreign Languages	Library Skills	Prereading	Physical Education	Authoring Systems	Word Processing	Typing Tutor	Business Education	Computer Literacy	Miscellaneous	Administration	Special Needs
Teacher's Pet Software 1517 Holly St. Berkeley, CA 94703 (415) 526-8068 PET	x	x																					
Teaching Pathways, Inc. P.O. Box 31582 Amarillo, TX 79120 (806) 373-1847 Apple II & III, TRS-80 I & III																							
Technical Language Systems, Inc. P.O. Box 172 San Angelo, TX 76902 (915) 655-0981 Apple	x	x	x						x	x	x		x		x		x				x		
Teck Associates P.O. Box 8732 White Bear Lake, MN 55110 (612) 429-5570 Apple																					x		
Temporal Activity Products Inc. 1535 121st Ave. S.E. Bellevue, WA 98005 (206) 746-2790 Apple								x															

Terrapin, Inc.
380 Green Street
Cambridge, MA 02139
(617) 492-8816
Apple

Texas Instruments
P.O. Box 53
Lubbock, TX 79408
(800) 858-4565
TI

The Micro Center
P.O. Box 6
Pleasantville, NY 11801
(516) 796-9392
Apple, Atari, Pet, TRS-80

The Professionals Workshop
1 Fletchers Mews, Neath Hill
Milton Keynes, Bucks
England
Apple II

The Programmers, Inc.
P.O. Box 1207
Taos, NM 87571
(505) 758-0576
Apple

The Psychological Corp.
757 Third Avenue
New York, NY 10017
(212) 888-3500
Apple, TRS-80

The Upper Room
907 6th Ave. E
Menomonie, WI 54751
(715) 235-5775
Apple, Texas Instruments

	Math	Language Arts	Reading	Spelling	Science	Social Studies	Geography	Basic Living Skills	Music	Art	Games	Foreign Languages	Library Skills	Prereading	Physical Education	Authoring Systems	Word Processing	Typing Tutor	Business Education	Computer Literacy	Miscellaneous	Administration	Special Needs
Thos. Wiggers, U. of MS Med. Cntr. 2500 N. State St. Jackson, MS 39206 (601) 987-5942 Apple																							
UNICOM 297 Elmwood Avenue Providence, RI 02907 (401) 467-5600 Apple																					x		
USE, Inc 14901 E. Hampden Ave. Suite 250 Denver, CO 80014 (303) 699-0438 Apple		x																			x		
Universal Systems For Ed. Inc. 14901 E. Hampden Ave, Suite 250 Aurora, CO 80014 (303) 699-0438 Apple II		x																					
Visual Horizens 180 Metro Park Rochester, NY 14623 (716) 424-5300 Apple																				x			

Wadsworth Electronic
Publishing Co.
20 Park Plaza
Boston, MA 02116
(800) 322-2208
Apple

Walt Woltosz
655 S. Fair Oaks, M213
Sunnyvale, CA 94086
(408) 733-6358
Apple II, TRS-80

Selected Software for Special Education

B

Software that may have applications for the Learning Disabled, Hearing Impaired, and Mentally Retarded

Drill and practice, tutorial and skill development programs for learning disabilities often come from materials produced for regular education. Many of the programs described in this appendix are such programs. They appear, from their producers' descriptions, to have qualities or features that could serve the needs of learning disabled students, hearing impaired, EMH, TMH, as well as those students with other specific learning disabilities. Other programs listed here have been created by special education producers. All of the program descriptions are those of the producers and are not intended to be product reviews.

Language Arts

Academics with Scanning LA
Apple II
$10.00

This program is designed for severely physically disabled students unable to use paper and pencil. Programs include *Word Attack, Cross-*

word, and *Phonics Machine*. The teacher types in word lists and the student then uses switches to produce work on the video screen or printer. A printer is not necessary, but is recommended.

> Computers to Help People, Inc.
> 1221 West Johnson Street
> Madison, WI 53715
> (608) 257-5917

Competency/Proficiency Assessment
Apple II, Commodore PET, and 64
$3,500 (estimate)

A comprehensive diagnostic, prescriptive and instructional series covering minimum skills in mathematics and language arts. Forty-six modules using over a hundred disks are expected in the math portion alone. Availability expected late 1983.

> Krell Software Corporation
> 1320 StonyBrook Rd
> Stony Brook, NY 11790
> (516) 751-5139

Computer Assistance Language Program
Apple II
$350.00

This program was developed with support from the Foundation For Children with Learning Disabilities and won a "Proud Project" award from that organization. Nine units cover nouns, verbs, adjectives, adverbs, pronouns, prepositions, conjunctions, interjections and subject-verb agreement. The instructional content focuses on morphology, syntax and semantics.

> Sysdata International, Inc.
> 7671 Old Central Avenue, NE
> Minneapolis, MN 55432
> (612) 780-1750

Diascriptive Reading
Apple, Atari, PET, TRS-80
$295.00, set of seven disks

A diagnostic, prescriptive, tutorial reading program covering main ideas, details, fact/opinion, vocabulary, sequence and inference at levels 3 to 8. The series contains six diagnostic tests and thirty-six developmental reading programs. The management system will keep track of the student's progress and will remediate or advance the student through each skill area without teacher intervention. Available on disk or cassette.

>Educational Activities, Inc.
>P.O. Box 392
>Freeport, NY 11520
>(800) 645-3739

First Categories
Apple II with Echo Speech Synthesizer
$120.00

An audible program that uses graphics, speech and text to train in six noun categories. The program was designed for beginning readers or learning disabled students. Requires Echo II Speech Synthesizer.

>Laureate Learning Systems, Inc.
>1 Mill Street
>Burlington, VT 05401
>(802) 862-7355

First Words
Apple II with Echo Speech Synthesizer
$185.00

A vocabulary comprehension training program which uses one hundred colorful pictures, animation and speech to teach children fifty essential nouns. There are six instructional levels. The program will accept input from single switch devices.

>Laureate Learning Systems, Inc.
>1 Mill Street
>Burlington, VT 05401
>(802) 862-7355

Language Arts Skill Builders
Apple II
$245.00, six disk set

Six different game formats with colorful graphics provide drill and practice in the following areas: word building through patterns, recognition of six parts of speech, subject-verb agreement, sight word recognition, and others. Speed, content and difficulty are all adjustable. Keyboard or paddle may be used for input. A special disk to make input easier through Scott Instrument's Shadow/Vet is also available. Individual programs are $44.00 each.

>Developmental Learning Materials
>One DLM Park
>Allen, TX 75002
>(214) 248-6300

Lessons in Syntax
Apple II Plus, 48K
$290.00, eight disk set

A tutorial language program teaching eight structures: negation, yes/no questions, wh-questions, because and so, relative clauses, participles, indirect discourse and passive voice. Animation and color are used to enhance interest. Students manipulate words and form sentences. Coordinated with a student workbook. A companion program is Dormac's *Test of Syntactic Ability*.

> Dormac, Inc.
> 8034 S.W. Nimbus
> Beaverton, OR 97005
> (800) 547-8032

Mastermatch
Apple
$39.95

In a TV quiz-show format, one or two players try to find logical matches in images and words under numbered mystery squares. Players use factual knowledge, visual memory and reasoning skills to win points. Many subject disks, beginning with Basic Skills (ages 4-7) are available at $19.95. The program also contains an authoring system so that special pictures, words or concepts may be entered.

> Computer Advanced Ideas, Inc.
> 1442A Walnut Street, Suite 341
> Berkeley, CA 94709
> (415) 526-9100

The Micro-Communicator
Apple II
$46.00

Individuals who have difficulty speaking or writing can now communicate with ease and speed. Users may draw upon prepared words and sentences, create their own sentences from common words stored in the computer, or combine words and sentences. Available in two versions: K-6 and 7 to adult.

> Scholastic Software
> 904 Sylvan Avenue
> Englewood Cliffs, NJ 07632
> (212) 944-7700

Microtyping II
Apple II+ or e, TRS-80, Atari
$29.95

Typing practice includes single letters, numbers and symbols; three letter words; sentences; computer program listings; and paragraphs. Up to thirty practice paragraphs can be created and saved for later practice. Words per minute and number of errors are displayed after each round; beeping noise signals error when it is made. Text editor allows editing of paragraphs and acquaints user with principles of word processing.

> Hayden Book Company, Inc.
> 600 Sussolk
> Lowell, MS 01853
> (800) 343-1218

PAL Reading Curriculum Packages
Apple II
$199.90

A reading diagnostic-remediation program that will diagnose the cause of reading problems and then provide remediation directly targeted to those problems. PAL covers the scope and sequence of reading education for each grade 2 through 6 and evaluates students' reading ability in up to forty major skills and 160 subskills. A master disk ($99.95) is required plus a curriculum package for each grade level ($99.95).

> Universal Systems For Education, Inc.
> 14901 East Hampden Avenue, Suite 250
> Aurora, CO 80014
> (303) 699-0438

The Pear Tree
Apple II
$40.00

Forty preprogrammed game files offer instruction in language arts, mathematics and reasoning skills. Includes an option for creating your own game files.

> Educational Computing Systems, Inc.
> 136 Fairbanks Road
> Oakridge, TN 37830
> (615) 483-4915

Primer 81
Apple II, Echo II Speech Synthesizer

For dyslexia and other related disorders these programs enable:

1. self-diagnosis of specific difficulties in letter recognition,
2. alteration of font and presentation time to improve discrimination,
3. instantaneous recognition training for common word and sentence structures,
4. motivation through rapid feedback and adaptive drills,
5. synthesized music with cadence synchronized visual presentation of lyrics (includes song editor).

> Bruce Land & David Farmer
> 395 Brooktondale Road
> Brooktondale, NY 14817

Quilt Letters
TRS-80 Model III, 48k
$69.95

Word game exercises to build vocabulary using three programs, *Quilt*, *Grid* and *Super-Six*. For junior high and high school levels. Players are presented letters by the computer and they must use them to create words. Built-in 2,400 word dictionary checks them for accuracy.

> Joseph Nichols Publisher
> P.O. Box 2394
> Tulsa, OK 74101
> (918) 583-3390

Reading Comprehension Games
Apple II
$499.50, 10 disk set

Short reading selections are presented at two reading levels, 2.0 to 3.5 (Red Level) or 3.5 to 5.0 (Blue Level). Subjects include: *Getting The Main Idea, Drawing Conclusions, Context Clues, Fact Or Opinion, Reading For Detail, Cause & Effect, Sequence, Inference, Following Directions* and *Alphabetizing*. Two to six students earn game points by correctly answering comprehension questions. Each program is available individually for $49.95.

> Learning Well
> 200 South Service Road
> Roslyn Heights, NY 11577
> (516) 621-1540

Reading Skills Series
Apple II, Atari, TI
$58.95 per pkg.

In the Texas Instrument version, speech, color graphics, animation and music combine to add interest and provide additional ports of entry for the course material. The Early Reading package benefits greatly from this. The series ranges from grades 1 to 6. Apple and Atari versions available in early 1984. These may not have complete speech in all packages.

    Scott, Foresman Electronic Publishing
    1900 East Lake Avenue
    Glenview, IL 60025
    (312) 729-3000

Talking Screen Textwriter
Apple II with Echo II Speech Synthesizer
$149.00

An elementary text editor is combined with the Echo Speech Synthesizer to allow easy vocalization of any text typed on the keyboard (or entered through keyboard emulators). Through simple commands the program will read or re-read text that has been typed. A part of the program will allow easy rewriting of the text to provide for proper pronunciation. The speech synthesizer must be purchased separately.

    School & Home Courseware, Inc.
    1341 Bulldog Lane, Suite C
    Fresno, CA 93710
    (209) 227-4341

VAKT '80
TRS-80 I/III, light pen, synthesizer
$29.95

This program simulates the visual, auditory, kenesthetic, tactile or multisensory reading techniques for learning disabled students. The student traces on a video screen using a light pen, while a voice synthesizer simultaneously "sounds out" proper letter-sound combinations of the words. Reading level is 3rd to 4th grade.

    Computers to Help People, Inc.
    1221 West Johnson Street
    Madison, WI 53715
    (608) 257-5917

The Vowels Tutorial
Apple II Plus
$120.00, three disk set

The student is presented with a visual stimulus such as r-t. Auditory instructions are given, such as type the missing letter you hear in the word "rat." If the student makes an error the program branches to a brief tutorial. Requires a Cassette Control Device from Hartley ($79.95) and cassette tape recorder for the audio delivery. Other programs with audio are available including authoring programs to create your own programs and audio tapes.

> Hartley Courseware, Inc.
> P.O. Box 431
> Dimondale, MI 48821
> (616) 942-8987

Wizard Of Words
Apple
$39.95

Five word games using knights, heralds, jugglers, a princess and a fire-breathing dragon create learning activities from a bank of 20,000 words in the program. An authoring system allows special lessons to be created. The games include completing words letter by letter, finding short words within a larger word, unjumbling words by placing letters in correct order, solving a crossword and trying to find a mystery word.

> Computer Advanced Ideas, Inc.
> 1442A Walnut Street, Suite 341
> Berkeley, CA 94709
> (415) 526-9100

Prereading

Early Counting Fun
Texas Instruments 99/4
$14.95

An extremely simple program to aid students who are having difficulty learning to count. Ducks, dogs, rabbits or a train can be presented on the screen and the child is taught to count up to nine. Objects may be of a similar type or mixed. The *Shark Counting* program provides a stronger game format. It requires the counting of gulls sitting on the ocean and pressing the proper key. Many helps can be selectively turned off to make the lesson harder.

>The Upper Room
>907 6th Avenue E
>Menomonie, WI 54751
>(715) 235-5775

Finger Painting
Apple II
$34.95

Finger Painting allows a child as young as three to finger paint in self-selected colors and background using total joystick control. The pictures can be saved on the child's own blank diskette. The menu is totally graphic; there are no words to read. A companion program is *Color Book I*, which takes over where *Finger Painting* leaves off. Children four years old and up use more complex painting techniques.

>Nova Software
>P.O. Box 545
>Alexandria, MN 56308
>(612) 762-8016

Juggles Rainbow
Apple II
$29.95

Juggles the clown helps prereaders learn reading and math readiness skills. In an entertaining game format, kids learn to relate horizontal to vertical planes, learn concepts of above and below, left and right, match colors, use words to give directions, recognize opposites, count, develop spatial awareness and recognize the shapes of "b," "d," "p" and "q," the four hardest letters in the alphabet.

>The Learning Company
>545 Middlefield Road, Suite 170
>Menlo Park, CA 94025
>(415) 328-5410

Keyboard Trainer
Texas Instruments 99/4
$15.00

The program has been designed to aid mentally handicapped students learn to use the computer keyboard. The program is designed to be very simple so that the student is not distracted by other activity on the screen. The activity is highly repetitious and structured.

> The Upper Room
> 907 6th Avenue E
> Menomonie, WI 54751
> (715) 235-5775

Kindergarten Primary
Commodore PET
$160, set of 10

Ten separate programs covering character, numeral, and shape identification. Greater than-less than concepts as well as same-different are taught. Many display in extremely large print on the screen. Some only require using the space bar to select correct answer. Others require pressing the key matching the correct answer. Each program in the set is available separately for $20. Available on cassette or disk.

> Comaldor
> P.O. Box 356, Postal Station O
> Toronto, Ontario
> Canada M4A 2N9
> (416) 751-7481

Mastermatch
Apple
$39.95

In a TV quiz-show format, one or two players try to find logical matches in images and words under numbered mystery squares. Players use factual knowledge, visual memory and reasoning skills to win points. Many subject disks, beginning with Basic Skills (ages 4 to 7) are available at $19.95. The program also contains an authoring system so that special pictures, words or concepts may be entered.

> Computer Advanced Ideas, Inc.
> 1442A Walnut Street, Suite 341
> Berkeley, CA 94709
> (415) 526-9100

Natural Voice Programs
Commodore PET or 64 with special recorder
$35.00 each

A special audio recorder ($225) allows natural voice instructions and helps to accompany the forty-seven programs offered by the company. Most are beginning skill programs for prereaders. The programs are also able to use input from a light pen ($38), also available from the company.

> Learning Tree Software, Inc.
> Box 246
> Kings Park, NY 11754
> (516) 462-6216

Pre-School IQ Builder 1 & 2
Apple II, Atari
$23.95

Decide whether pairs of figures are the same or different. Match the letter on the screen with the letter on the keyboard. In 2, move the letter, number or symbol to the bottom of the screen to cover its mate and the screen will sing a happy song. Both programs for ages 3 to 6. Atari versions: 16K cassette ($16.95) and 24K disk ($23.95).

> Program Design, Inc.
> 11 Idar Court
> Greenwich, CT 06830
> (203) 661-8799

Special Skill Builder I
Apple II, Atari
$29.95

Four programs offer development of early skills. Limited keyboard skills or the game paddles can be used for the answers. Shapes or colors can be matched with samples displayed, shapes can be counted or numerals can be matched with the spelled number. A management program allows the teacher to change the number of the problems presented, turn sound on or off, keep track of responses and vary the speed of presentation.

> Quality Educational Software
> P.O. Box 502
> Troy, MI 48099
> (313) 689-5059

Special Skill Builder II
Apple II, Atari
$29.95

Four programs are available. In *Alpha Drill*, an upper case letter is displayed at the top of the screen and the student must match it against randomly displayed lower case letters. *Alphabet Line* asks the student to fill in a missing letter in a section of alphabet. *Number Line* does the same with numerals. *Inside Out* teaches those concepts. Game controllers or the keyboard can be used for input.

>Quality Educational Software
>P.O. Box 502
>Troy, MI 48099
>(313) 689-5059

The Talking Alphabet
Apple II
$24.95

The Talking Alphabet teaches children the alphabet in both cases, to recognize letters by name, to print upper and lower case letters and to recognize, count and print numbers. Voice synthesis and color graphics allows a child of four to practice on his own. The voice is built into the program, and it is not necessary to purchase an additional speech synthesizer.

>Nova Software
>P.O. Box 545
>Alexandria, MN 56308
>(612) 762-8016

Math

Academics with Scanning
Apple II Plus
$10.00

For students unable to use pencil and paper. Programs do not instruct students in math tasks but do allow them to use the computer as a writing aid. Problems and/or worksheets are first typed in by the teacher/helper, and then student uses one or two switches to produce video and paper outputs. Appropriate for grades 3 to 7. Printer not necessary, but recommended.

>Computers to Help People, Inc.
>1221 West Johnson Street
>Madison, WI 53715
>(608) 257-5917

Basic Math Competency Skill Drills
Apple, Atari, PET, TRS-80
$203.00, set of six disks

The very large type used in the screen display of math problems may make these programs especially useful for vision impaired students.

The drills are at the Junior-Senior High level for basic operations. Each disk is available separately at $39.95. Cassettes are available for some of the systems at $173.00 for the set or $15.95 per cassette.

> Educational Activities, Inc.
> P.O. Box 392
> Freeport, NY 11520
> (800) 645-3739

Bumble Games
Apple II
$39.95

Kids learn numbers through ten and how to use number pairs to name positions on a grid. Plotting number pairs is a necessary skill to understand and build charts and graphs and to locate places on a map. Designed for kids aged four to ten. Companion program *Bumble Plot* carries these skills onward using positive and negative numbers to name points on four quadrant grids. Music and sound effects can be turned off.

> The Learning Company
> 545 Middlefield Road, Suite 170
> Menlo Park, CA 94025
> (415) 328-5410

Competency/Proficiency Assessment
Apple II, Commodore PET, 64
$3,500 (estimate)

A comprehensive diagnostic, prescriptive and instructional series covering minimum skills in mathematics and language arts. Forty-six modules using over one hundred disks expected in the math portion alone. Availability expected late 1983.

> Krell Software Corporation
> 1320 Stony Brook Road
> Stony Brook, NY 11790
> (516) 751-5139

Edufun Series
Apple II, Atari
$39.95 each

A series of twelve programs using a game format including extensive graphics and animation. The programs were developed under a National Science Foundation project based on a "Position Statement Of Basic Skills" released by the National Council of Supervisors of

Mathematics. Each activity provides practice and enrichment in one or more of these basic skill areas.

>Milliken Publishing Company
>1100 Research Boulevard
>St. Louis, MO 63132
>(314) 991-4220

Gertrude's Secrets
Apple II
$44.95

Gertrude's Secrets helps kids to think logically, create order and plan ahead. Kids move puzzle pieces and guess secret rules to solve puzzles. They can also create their own puzzle pieces. Designed for ages four to nine. A companion program *Gertrude's Puzzles* expands upon these skills by having the kids solve complex puzzles, sometimes with a minimum of clues.

>The Learning Company
>545 Middlefield Road, Suite 170
>Menlo Park, CA 94025
>(415) 328-5410

Microaddition
Apple II+ or e, Atari tape or disk
$29.95

Animated visual aids and auditory reinforcement with familiar children's songs are used to teach basic counting and addition skills. A help option uses graphic aids to convey the principles of addition. The program has four levels of difficulty, supplies the right answer after three incorrect answers, and uses color to differentiate between right and wrong answers. Familiar objects are used first before numbers are introduced. Ages 4-10.

>Hayden Book Company, Inc.
>600 Sussolk
>Lowell, MS 01853
>(800) 343-1218

Microdivision
Apple II+ or e, Atari tape or disk
$29.95

Animated visual aids and auditory reinforcement are used to teach basic counting and division skills to ages 4-10. Familiar objects are used first before numbers are introduced. Both evenly divisible and numbers with remainders are used. Help option uses graphics to convey basic principles. Provides four levels of difficulty. Supplies correct answer after three incorrect attempts.

>Hayden Book Company, Inc.
>600 Sussolk
>Lowell, MS 01853
>(800) 343-1218

Micromultiplication
Apple II+ or e, Atari tape or disk
$29.95

Animated visual aids and auditory reinforcement are used to teach basic counting and multiplication skills to ages 4-10. Familiar objects are used first before numbers are introduced. The program has four levels of difficulty, and help option uses graphics to convey basic principles. Correct answer supplied after three incorrect attempts. Tallies right and wrong answers.

>Hayden Book Company, Inc.
>600 Sussolk
>Lowell, MS 01853
>(800) 343-1218

Microsubtraction
Apple II+ or e, Atari tape or disk
$29.95

Animated visual aids and auditory reinforcements are used to teach basic counting and subtraction skills. For ages 4-10, students work first with familiar objects before numbers are introduced. A help option uses graphics to convey basic principles. Program has four levels of difficulty, and supplies correct answer after three incorrect attempts. Shows how to borrow from the tens place. Tallies right and wrong answers.

>Hayden Book Company, Inc.
>600 Sussolk
>Lowell, MS 01853
>(800) 343-1218

Micro Math
Apple II, Atari
$29.95 each

Separate programs for addition, subtraction, multiplication and division are aimed at the four to ten year old. Familiar objects such as birds or balloons are first used to develop concepts and reinforce counting skills. Operations are shown step by step and then the child has an opportunity to do a problem. Atari version available on either tape or disk.

>Hayden Book Company, Inc.
>600 Sussolk
>Lowell, MS 01853
>(800) 343-1218

Musical Math
Atari 16K tape or 32K disk
$34.95

Addition, subtraction, multiplication and division practice are all on this disk, for preschool ages through adult. The program keeps score and uses ten familiar children's songs as reinforcement. The game may be re-started at different levels of difficulty.

>Hayden Book Company, Inc.
>600 Sussolk
>Lowell, MS 01853
>(800) 343-1218

Personal Mathematics
Apple II, TRS-80
$55.00, set of two

Practical mathematical skills are introduced and taught with a simplified real life approach. Each program has a testing and student management section. Program titles are: *Real Cost: Is A Sale Really A Sale?* and *Fractions, Percents And Decimals Using Everyday Examples*. The programs are available individually at $29.95. TRS-80 programs available both on cassette and disk.

>Aquarius Publishers, Inc.
>P.O. Box 128
>Indian Rocks Beach, FL 33535
>(813) 595-7890

Problem Solving
Commodore PET
$90, set of six

A set of six tapes or disks that allow a student to enter problems of his choice. The program checks the student's work, step by step.

>Comaldor
>P.O. Box 356, Postal Station O
>Toronto, Ontario
>Canada M4A 2N9
>(416) 751-7481

Rocky's Boots
Apple II
$49.95

Rocky's Boots will help kids develop logic skills while gaining an understanding of electronics. The kids work with elements in the program to build working machines that score game points. While building the machines, kids learn about computer logic circuits. The main function of the program is to expand reasoning and problem solving skills.

>The Learning Company
>545 Middlefield Road, Suite 170
>Menlo Park, CA 94025
>(415) 328-5410

Special Skill Builder I
Apple II, Atari
$29.95

Four programs offer development of early skills. Limited keyboard skills or the game paddles can be used for the answers. Shapes or colors can be matched with samples displayed, shapes can be counted or numerals can be matched with the spelled number. A management program allows the teacher to change the number of the problems presented, turn sound on and off, keep track of responses and vary the speed of presentation.

>Quality Educational Software
>P.O. Box 502
>Troy, MI 48099
>(313) 689-5059

Miscellaneous

Bowling Series
Apple II+
$85.00

A three disk set that offers comprehensive instruction and skill analysis for bowling. Includes equipment selection; animation of the four step approach and concepts involved in various ball deliveries; a tutorial on scoring symbols and rules, including scoring a simulated game; an introduction to spot bowling techniques; and a simulation involving spare conversion strategies. Demo program available for $15.00.

>Project REACT
>66 Malcolm Ave. SE
>Minneapolis, MN 55414
>(612) 379-0428

Graphics Machine
Atari 800
$19.95

This is not an authoring system, but a graphics program that allows easier creation of graphics material which may later be used with any authoring system that allows the use of shapes tables. Graphics are done in mode 8 with 3 colors, and text can be put almost anywhere on the screen. 48k required.

> Educational Software, Inc.
> 4565 Cherryvale
> Soquel, CA 95073
> (408) 476-4901

Heart and Exercise
Apple II+
$30.00

Four programs instruct the student on how the heart works and how exercise affects it. *The Magnificent Machine* introduces the anatomy of the heart, the role of the arteries and veins, and the affect of exercise on the heart. *Pulse* introduces the pulse and how to take a pulse rate. *Exercise Your Way To Good Health* shows how the heart is affected by various sports activities and helps to design a personal cardiovascular fitness program.

> Project REACT
> 66 Malcolm Ave. SE
> Minneapolis, MN 55414
> (612) 379-0428

Music Major
Atari 32K tape or disk
$39.95

A series of programs to help the beginning music student learn more about the fundamentals of music. It gives comprehensive lessons on keyboard and note recognition, note counting, measure practice, key signatures and a utility to write your own quizzes.

> Educational Software, Inc.
> 4565 Cherryvale
> Soquel, CA 95073
> (408) 476-4901

Orienteering Series
Apple II+
$120.00 per set

Programs include: Nature's direction finders (direction by sun and stars), parts of the compass, plotting a bearing, compass function, procedures for compass reading, map reading, scale, map symbols, and an adventure simulation reinforcing the above orienteering skills. The game paddles are used to manipulate compass readings and bearings. Six disks. Individual disks are available at $30.00 each.

> Project REACT
> 66 Malcolm Ave. SE
> Minneapolis, MN 55414
> (612) 379-0428

The S.A.M. Tutorial
Atari
$29.95

A tutorial covering expanded use of the software automated mouth, a software based speech synthesizer available from *Don't Ask Software*. Covers emphasizing words, singing, and combining graphics with voice. Requires S.A.M. and 32k Atari.

> Educational Software, Inc.
> 4565 Cherryvale
> Soquel, CA 95073
> (408) 476-4901

Sports Terminology Series
Apple II+
$20.00 each

Programs to learn and reinforce sports vocabulary and definitions. Volume 1 includes individual, dual and team sports; Volume 2 includes aquatic sports; volume 3 includes swimming and rescue; Volume 4 includes winter sports.

> Project REACT
> 66 Malcolm Ave. SE
> Minneapolis, MN 55414
> (612) 379-0428

Volleyball Series
Apple II+
$15.00

A three-disk package that offers comprehensive instruction and skill analysis for volleyball. Includes court anatomy, player positions, rules, officiating techniques, and skill fundamentals. Includes animation and simulations that instruct and analyze the underhand and overhand serve, bump, set and spike. A simulation of a game requires the student to indicate what the official's call should be.

>Project REACT
>66 Malcolm Ave. SE
>Minneapolis, MN 55414
>(612) 379-0428

Physically Handicapped
C

Programs and modifications have been created for use by physically handicapped individuals and more are created each day. This appendix is only a partial listing of programs currently available for the nonverbal, profoundly motor-handicapped.

Many of the programs listed are from the Trace Center International Software/Hardware Registry. The Trace Research and Development Center, University of Wisconsin gathers and publishes the Registry under a grant from Cerebral Palsy, Inc. and the National Institute of Handicapped Research, U.S. Department of Education.

Academics with Scanning
Apple II Plus
$10.00

For students unable to use pencil and paper. Programs do not instruct students in math tasks but do allow them to use the computer as a writing aid. Problems and/or worksheets are first typed in by the teacher/helper, and then the student uses one or two switches to produce video and paper outputs. Appropriate for grades 3 to 7. Printer not necessary, but recommended.

    Computers to Help People. Inc.
    1221 West Johnson Street
    Madison, WI 53715
    (608) 257-5917

Academics with Scanning LA
Apple II
$10.00

This program is designed for severely physically disabled students unable to use paper and pencil. Programs include *Word Attack*, *Crossword*, and *Phonics Machine*. The teacher types in word lists and the student then uses switches to produce work on the video screen or printer. Printer not necessary, but recommended.

> Computers to Help People, Inc.
> 1221 West Johnson Street
> Madison, WI 53715
> (608) 257-5917

Blissymbolics
Apple II
$161.00

These three packages allow a person to learn and use the Bliss symbolic language for nonvocal disabled people. *Bliss Drills* is a series of drills to learn the language ($32). *Bliss Library*, three disks, provides the 1500 symbols used for communications. ($95.) Blissboard puts the user in control of 500 symbols that can be displayed on the screen or printed on paper ($34.) All of the programs will accept input from special switches.

> MECC (Minn. Ed. Comp. Consortium)
> 2520 Broadway Drive
> St. Paul, MN 55113
> (612) 638-0627

Communi-Mate
PET, CBM
$100.00

Using switch input, complete word processing including editing can be done. The program will also store words and phrases that can be inserted into the text. The material may then be formatted by the program and sent to the printer for output. Available on both tape and disk.

> Green Valley Informantics
> 769 North Sacre Lane
> Monmouth, OR 97361
> (503) 838-1172

Dots and Draw
Apple II
$25.00

Allows the user to draw pictures by "join the dots." Single switch input or input from paddle or joystick. A library of thirty dot pictures plus thirty words in large letters is included. An additional disk of forty more dot pictures is available for $30.00.

> The Professional Workshop
> 1 Fletchers Mews, Neath Hill
> Milton Keynes, Bucks
> England

EZBAS
Apple II Plus
$50.00

This program allows the profoundly motor-handicapped to program and control the computer using an alternative input device, single, dual, triple, quad, or quint switches. All words, symbols, phrases, and numbers needed to program and control the Apple II are displayed on "pages" in the top four-fifths of the screen. As the program or instructions are chosen from the page displayed, they are added to the listing.

> I.O.R. Enterprises
> Route 6, Box 20
> Chapel Hill, NC 27514
> (919) 929-4825

Florida Scanner
Apple II
$45.00

This program assists a programmer in modifying certain standard Applesoft keyboard entry programs to be operated by a single switch connected through the game controller port. Included is an input finder that displays or prints out all keyboard input statements in the program, the Florida Scanner subroutine which is added to the program, and a sample single switch game.

> G. Evan Rushakoff
> New Mexico State University
> Las Cruces, NM 88003
> (505) 646-2801

Handicapped Typewriter
Apple II
$200.00

A single switch can operate this text printing system. A keyboard is displayed on the screen and a scanning cursor allows selection of the letter. Also included is a user definable word and phrase dictionary, a calculator, a telephone answering, dialing and directory service, and an environmental control system. All may be controlled by a single switch. An Introl X-10 control system is required.

>Rocky Mountain Software, Inc.
>214-131 Water Street
>Vancouver, B.C.
>Canada V6B 4M3

Insta-Speak
TRS-80 I, PMC-80
$30.00

This is for nonverbal individuals to type phonetically via keyboard and then output speech. Comes with keyboard labels for English phonemes. Screen displays the phonetic message as it is typed. Pressing Speak key outputs the message via the synthesizer which must be part of the hardware system. *Insta-Print* (another program by the author) will be included at no extra cost, if requested.

>I.O.R. Enterprises
>Route 6, Box 20
>Chapel Hill, NC 27514
>(919) 929-4825

Micro Communicator
Apple II or II Plus
$48.00

A single keystroke by finger or mouth stick will display any sentence chosen from sixty or more programmed sentences which can be changed at anytime by the user. Messages of up to one hundred words and phrases can be used. A built-in vocabulary of 1600 words for each letter of the alphabet, more than 250 words listed by categories, and a 50-word list of user-changeable words and phrases are available.

>Grover and Associates
>7 Mt. Lassen Drive D116
>San Rafael, CA 94903
>(415) 479-5906

Motor-Handicapped Support System
Heath/Zenith H-89
$499.00

This is a hardware/software system designed to be plug-in compatible with standard microcomputers. It provides the handicapped person with voice-recognition access to the communications and control capabilities of the micro, control of peripherals, and interface to special purpose equipment. Plans to convert to Radio Shack, Apple and S-100 systems are underway.

>Artra Inc.
>P.O. Box 653
>Arlington, VA 22216
>(703) 527-0455

Motor Training Games
Apple II Plus
$10.00

Disk includes thirteen different motor training games designed to allow practice using one or two switches. Appropriate for preschool through teen years or higher.

>Computers to Help People, Inc.
>1221 West Johnson Street
>Madison, WI 53715
>(608) 257-5917

N.U. Communication & Device Controller
Apple II
$285.00

With two switch input, text may be created and edited, saved and printed or transmitted. The keyboard is bypassed, switches are connected through the game controller port. Appliances, the telephone and a printer can also be controlled by using BSR home controller receivers.

>Prentke Romich Company
>8769 Township Road 513
>Shreve, OH 44676
>(216) 567-2906

Picture-Com
Apple II Plus
$40.00

For the nonverbal, profoundly motor-handicapped individual who cannot read English. Seven (or more) screen pages with sixteen pictures per screen. Blissymbols and Pictograms are available. Input technique can be one of twenty variations of switch interface. As each picture is chosen, the English equivalent is printed at the bottom of the video screen.

    I.O.R. Enterprises
    Route 6, Box 20
    Chapel Hill, NC 27514
    (919) 929-4825

Public Domain Software
Apple II
No charge

Many public domain educational programs have been modified to run under single switch scanning control. A brief description of the programs is available. To order, send up to eighteen blank disks plus enough stamps or cash for return postage. The project also welcomes the contribution of public domain software.

    Project C.A.I.S.H., Gocio Elementary School
    3450 Gocio Road
    Sarasota, FL 33580
    (813) 355-3567

Quick-Scan
TRS-80 I/III
$30.00

This is a communications device for the nonverbal individual. Single switch control of cursor to choose alphabet, punctuation and control words. As each letter is chosen it is added to the text below. The text is easily edited. Once satisfied with the text, the user can output it easily to the printer. Tape based, the program needs a printer.

    I.O.R. Enterprises
    Route 6, Box 20
    Chapel Hill, NC 27514
    (919) 929-4825

Say It
Apple II, speech synthesizer
$30.00

This is a talking program operated by a single switch that stores phrases. The phrase may have a "blank" or word missing, which is then filled in from a menu of possible choices. Once the phrase is completed it is output through a speech synthesizer. The phrases on the program may be modified or replaced.

>Carl Geigner
>1603 Court Street
>Syracuse, NY 13208

Single Switch Assessment Program
Apple II
$40.00

Provides mean "normal response time" for activation of single switches. To be used in determining what type of switch is best suited for a particular individual.

>G. Evan Rushakoff
>New Mexico State University
>Las Cruces, NM 88003
>(505) 646-2801

Single Switch Game Library
Apple II

A variety of games have been modified to work with the Florida Scanner program which is included on the disk. The entire disk, including the menu, is able to be operated by single switch control. Contact the developer for information on specific games available and prices.

>G. Evan Rushakoff
>New Mexico State University
>Las Cruces, NM 88003
>(505) 646-2801

Speaking Comm/Control Device
TRS-80 I, PMC-80
$225.00

This program is a speech or printing output communication device for the nonverbal, profoundly motor-handicapped. A single switch controls the speed of the cursor for choice of words or phrases on screen. Satisfied with the message, the user can "print" or "speak" the message. Environmental control by choosing command is included, with alarms. Additional equipment is the speech synthesizer and TRS-80 Plug 'N Power module. Printer is optional.

>I.O.R. Enterprises
>Route 6, Box 20
>Chapel Hill, NC 27514
>(919) 929-4825

Special Inputs Disk
Apple II Plus
$10.00

This is a utilities disk for special input devices. Single switch scanning, regular or step, Morse code and assisted keyboard routines are included. Load the input method first, then use that method to run programs designed for keyboard entry. Some commercial or off-the-shelf disks may be run with *special inputs*, though some modifications in these programs may be required (instructions are included).

>Computers to Help People, Inc.
>1221 West Johnson Street
>Madison, WI 53715
>(608) 257-5917

Special Needs, Volume 1
Apple II
$34.95

Twenty drills covering primary spelling words are contained on this disk. In each drill a sentence with three possible choices is presented to the student. A box will move over each choice. Students should press the game paddle button, turn the knob or hit any key on the keyboard when the box is over the correct answer. Any type of special switch can be connected through the game paddle.

>MECC (Minn. Ed. Comp. Consortium)
>2520 Broadway Drive
>St. Paul, MN 55113
>(612) 638-0627

Special Needs, Volume 2
Apple II
$34.95

A moving box scans each possible answer on each program. The keyboard, a game paddle or special switches can select the correct answer. On this disk is a drill on the four basic arithmetic operations, a drill on making change, a music program titled *Wrong Note* and two programs simulating the food web, *Odel Woods* and *Odel Lake*.

> MECC (Minn. Ed. Comp. Consortium)
> 2520 Broadway Drive
> St. Paul, MN 55113
> (612) 638-0627

Talking Blissapple
Apple II
$35.00

This program allows individuals who use Blissymbols to have a means of writing. The program turns the Apple into a talking typewriter for Blissymbols. Supports custom vocabulary development. It displays, prints, or speaks symbol messages at user's command. Optional equipment includes a Vodex for voice, Silentype printer, and SSM AIO serial/parallel board for interfacing to other communication aids.

> Computers to Help People, Inc.
> 1221 West Johnson Street
> Madison, WI 53715
> (608) 257-5917

Voice Based Learning System
Apple II with Shadow/VET
$99.95

The *Voice Based Learning System* allows a student to use voice or sound to input answers to specially created instructional material. The program is an authoring system that allows the creation of individualized material without learning a programming language. Voice entry is through the Shadow/VET, produced by Scott Instruments ($995.00). The voice entry system is trained to recognize each individual's speech or repeatable sounds.

> Sterling Swift Publishing Co.
> 1600 Fortview Rd.
> Austin, TX 78704
> (512) 444-7570

Words +
Apple II, TRS-80
$75.00

Stored words and phrases are used to build sentences and messages which can be saved on disk or printed out. Other features include drawing, games, reading articles, calculator, telephone interface and appliance control. New features are frequently added to the program. All modes use a single switch with scan or two switch operation.

>Walt Woltosz
>655 S. Fair Oaks, M213
>Sunnyvale, CA 94086
>(408) 733-6358

Blind

D

The number of microcomputer programs to aid the blind and vision impaired are growing. This appendix is just a partial listing of some of the special programs designed to generate speech or grade II Braille with a microcomputer.

Braille-Edit
Apple II, two disk drives
$250.00

A text editing program for the Apple that translates English text to grade II Braille and reverse translates grade II Braille to English text. The program will work with a Versabraille paperless Brailler as well as many modified printers to produce Braille on paper. It also prints English text on standard printers. Two disks providing extensive information about the program and devices it supports are available for $20.

    Raised Dot Computing
    310 South 7th Street
    Lewisburg, PA 17837
    (717) 523-6739

Braille Training Program
Apple II
$200.00

This program teaches and drills sighted persons in grade II Braille. Rules and contractions are displayed on the television screen. The user is presented with sample text to enter in Braille. The Apple keyboard acts like a Braillewriter and displays the entered Braille cells on the monitor. When the drill is ended, the computer compares the entered material with the correct version and displays any errors.

> Raised Dot Computing
> 310 South 7th Street
> Lewisburg, PA 17837
> (717) 523-6739

Duxbury Braille Translator
North Star & other CP/M
$985

Text to grade 2 Braille translator with tables for American English, British English and Spanish. Price for individual non-commercial use is $985. General non-commercial license is $4,340. Commercial licenses are available. Duxbury also produces a variety of complete systems including computers, voice output and Braille embossers. Consulting services are also available.

> Duxbury Systems, Inc
> 77 Great Road
> Acton, MA 07120
> (617) 263-7761

Ed-It Text Editor
Apple II
$100

A line-oriented Braille text editor. The Apple keyboard functions as a six-key Braille keyboard. The Braille cells are displayed on the screen and may be edited. The program will drive a Braille embosser with an appropriate interface card.

> Robert E. Stepp III
> Station A, P.O. Box 5002
> Champaign, IL 61820
> (217) 359-7933

The Electronic Blackboard
Apple II
$80.00

The Apple keyboard will emulate a Braillewriter and allow the input of text and math equations. The material is instantly translated to English text and displayed on the screen. The program is designed to allow a blind person to present text and equations to a sighted audience. The program will store several screens of information and can print on a special dot matrix printer.

>Raised Dot Computing
>310 South 7th Street
>Lewisburg, PA 17837
>(717) 523-6739

Executive Secretary
IBM PC
$200.00 (est.)

A powerful word processing program has been combined with the Echo GP speech synthesizer from Street Electronics, to provide speech output or display of all material entered. The user may move an audio cursor around the screen to voice lines, words, or complete paragraphs. Speech synthesizer needed at an additional cost of approximately $300.00.

>Sof/Sys, Inc.
>4306 Upyon Avenue South
>Minneapolis, MN 55410
>(612) 929-7104

O-Column Mathematics
Apple II, two disk drives
$200.00

An option to the *Braille-Edit* program that allows the user to write text and mathematical equations on the VersaBraille and have the material printed on a special dot matrix printer. The program can use the Nemeth code for writing Braille mathematics and can also translate grade II text.

>Raised Dot Computing
>310 South 7th Street
>Lewisburg, PA 17837
>(717) 523-6739

Talking Screen Textwriter
Apple II with Echo II Speech Synthesizer
$149.00

An elementary text editor is combined with the Echo Speech Synthesizer to allow easy vocalization of any text typed on the keyboard (or entered through keyboard emulators). Through simple commands the program will read or reread text that has been typed. A part of the program will allow easy rewriting of the text to provide for proper pronunciation. The speech synthesizer must be purchased separately.

School & Home Courseware, Inc.
1341 Bulldog Lane, Suite C
Fresno, CA 93710
(209) 227-4341

Authoring Systems
E

Authoring systems are programs to help teachers and parents create lessons for use on the microcomputer. With authoring systems such as those listed in this appendix, it's possible to create individualized lesson materials for the exact needs of the student. They are easy to use and require no programming experience.

The Adaptable Skeleton
Apple II
$34.95

The teacher enters multiple choice questions. Up to four answer choices are allowed. The teacher can enter a brief feedback message associated to each answer choice. The teacher can also have a review screen be shown to a student each time a particular answer is chosen. In the drill mode students can select the number of questions to answer, in the quiz mode the teacher selects the number of questions.

>Micro Power & Light Company
>12820 Hillcrest Road, Suite 224
>Dallas, TX 75230
>(214) 239-6620

Assisted Instructional Development System
Apple II
$395.00

A special card which plugs into the Apple combines with software to allow a teacher to create custom courseware with no programming knowledge. Branching can be done to three levels. The lessons can be timed or presented without time limit. A management system allows the generation of reports on student progress.

    Skillcorp Software
    1711 McGaw Avenue
    Irvine, CA 92714
    (800) 845-8688

CAIWARE 3D
TRS-80
$219.00

Formatted screens may include text and graphics. Some graphics generation is possible through arrow key manipulation. Question screens allow multiple choice, true/false or fill-in answers. Lessons may be copied from disk to tape for use on 16K tape systems. Author may provide for branching to remedial work if student performance is low. *SUPER-CAI* is similar, but is tape based for 16K systems and sells for $64.95.

    Fireside Computing, Inc.
    5843 Montgomery Road
    Elkridge, MD 21227
    (301) 796-4165

Electric English Authoring
Apple II
$99.95, three disk set

Electric English is available as a two disk set with a complete instructional program covering parts of speech, phrases, and clauses ($74.95). If you wish to modify the program to meet special needs or fit into a specific teaching style, the three disk authoring system provides this capability. It is possible to make small modifications or rewrite all of the screens. A 200-page manual accompanies the author program.

    TIES
    1925 W. County Road B2
    St. Paul, MN 55113
    (612) 633-9100

Eureka Learning System
Apple II
$495.00

The *Text Writer* portion of the system allows the author to create text materials of their choice. An *Illustrator File* contains special math, music and other symbols for inclusion in the lesson. A *Shape Editor* allows the inclusion of graphics. Fee quoted is for license on one computer system. License for additional systems is $49.50 each. Extensive support and future revisions are included.

> Eiconics, Inc.
> P.O. Box 1207, 211 Cruz Alta Road
> Taos, NM 87571
> (505) 758-1696

E-Z PILOT
Apple II
$49.95

The twelve commands in E-Z PILOT allow a person to create complete interactive courseware on any subject. Color, sound and large size alphabets can also be used. Graphics or other programs in BASIC can be inserted anywhere in the course materials.

> Teck Associates
> P.O. Box 8732
> White Bear Lake, MN 55110
> (612) 429-5570

Individual Study Center
Apple II, TRS-80 Mod I & III
$69.95

Drill-and-practice questions can be created by a teacher and then run as part of up to eight different game formats. Prepared questions are also available in the following subjects: basic math, biology, English, geography, history, languages and spelling. Programs are available on disk or tape, depending on the system.

> Teach Yourself By Computer Software
> 2128 West Jefferson Road
> Pittsford, NY 14534
> (716) 424-5453

Light Pen Quiz
Apple II Plus with light pen
$49.95

A general purpose teaching program that allows the teacher to create his own CAI quizzes. Students may use a light pen which is also produced by the company ($79.95) as their input tool in answering the quiz.

>CMA (Charles Mann and Associates)
>55722 Santa Fe Trail
>Yucca Valley, CA 92284
>(619) 365-9718

Mastermatch
Apple
$39.95

In a TV quiz-show format, one or two players try to find logical matches in images and words under numbered mystery squares. Players use factual knowledge, visual memory and reasoning skills to win points. Many subject disks, beginning with *Basic Skills* (ages 4 to 7) are available at $19.95. The program also contains an authoring system so that special pictures, words or concepts may be entered.

>Computer Advanced Ideas, Inc.
>1442A Walnut Street, Suite 341
>Berkeley, CA 94709
>(415) 526-9100

Microteach
Apple II, Atari 800
$275

This two disk system is comprised of the *Teachers Aide*, which allows creation of the courseware, and *Student Pak*, which allows the student to run the courseware without being able to modify it. Text may be presented as pages, or the text may be scrolled. The time a page is displayed is controlled by the author. The system always provides menus of available options. It is available in English or Spanish.

>Compumax, Inc.
>P.O. Box 7239
>Menlo Park, CA 94025
>(415) 854-6700

Phonics, Text, & Graphics
Apple II Plus
$10.00

A unique program that can be used with a special inputs disk to allow scanning, Morse code, or assisted keyboard entry. The user can write, edit, save, and print or draw. A teacher may use *Worksheet Writer* to type material for the student's own level. A utilities program allows copying of disk and initializing of auxiliary disks for storage of text, drawings, and worksheets. For use with *Special Inputs*, switches can be substituted for game buttons.

>Computers to Help People, Inc.
>1221 West Johnson Street
>Madison, WI 53715
>(608) 257-5917

TRS-80 Author I
TRS-80 Model I & III, disk
$149.95

A screen oriented authoring system that features full screen editing, graphics, branching, score keeping, hints and more.

>Radio Shack (Education Division)
>1600 Tandy Center
>Fort Worth, TX 76102
>(817) 390-3302

Using A Calendar
Apple II
$39.95

A picture of a calendar page is presented, along with information or a question. The *Create* feature of the program allows the teacher to enter his own information or questions. A companion program is *Calendar Skills* ($29.95) that includes drill on days of the week and months of the year. *Create* also allows the use of teacher created material in this program.

>Hartley Courseware, Inc.
>P.O. Box 431
>Dimondale, MI 48821
>(616) 942-8987

Vanilla Pilot
Commodore
$29.95

A tape-based authoring system for most Commodore microcomputers. Just a few commands allow creation of interactive courseware without learning a programming language. Keyboard graphics may be included and you can switch between dark type on a white screen and the standard light type on a dark background.

> Tamarack Software
> P.O. Box 247
> Darby, MT 59829
> (406) 821-4596

Vocabulary Prompter
Apple II
$29.95

Allows the development of word or phrase lists for vocabulary drill or testing. Can also be used for mathematics drills. The presentation format is fixed but the information presented is controlled by the author. Also available is *Super Prompter* which presents material in Russian Cyrillic or Japanese Katakana.

> Jagdstaffel Software
> 608 Blossom Hill Road
> San Jose, CA 95123
> (408) 578-1643

Voice Based Learning System
Apple II with Shadow/VET
$99.95

The *Voice Based Learning System* allows a student to use voice or sound to input answers to specially created instructional material. The program is an authoring system that allows the creation of individualized material without learning a programming language. Voice entry is through the Shadow/VET, produced by Scott instruments ($995.00). The voice entry system is trained to recognize each individual's speech or repeatable sounds.

> Sterling Swift Publishing Co.
> 1600 Fortview Rd.
> Austin, TX 78704
> (512) 444-7570

The Vowels Tutorial
Apple II Plus
$120.00, three disk set

The student is presented with a visual stimulus such as r-t. Auditory instructions are given, such as type the missing letter you hear in the word "rat." If the student makes an error the program branches to a brief tutorial. Requires a Cassette Control Device from Hartley ($79.95) and cassette tape recorder for the audio delivery. Other programs with audio are available including authoring programs to create your own programs and audio tapes.

> Hartley Courseware, Inc.
> P.O. Box 431
> Dimondale, MI 48821
> (616) 942-8987

Wizard of Words
Apple
$39.95

Five word games using knights, heralds, jugglers, a princess and a fire-breathing dragon create learning activities from a bank of 20,000 words in the program. An authoring system allows special lessons to be created. The games include completing words letter by letter, finding short words within a larger word, unjumbling words by placing letters in correct order, solving a crossword and trying to find a mystery word.

> Computer Advanced Ideas, Inc.
> 1442A Walnut Street, Suite 341
> Berkeley, CA 94709
> (415) 526-9100

Word Wise
Apple II
$74.95

An authoring system producing drill-and-practice questions. The students either fill in a blank in a sentence or match a word or phrase with a picture. Text materials may be presented in standard text size on the screen or in a one-inch high character set. A companion series, *Picture Library* consists of twenty-nine disks of approximately 1,000 images which may be used with *Word Wise. Picture Library* costs $324.95.

> TIES
> 1925 W. County Road B2
> St. Paul, MN 55113
> (612) 633-9100

Administration
F

The programs listed in this appendix include clinical and diagnostic software as well as management systems for such administrative uses as Individual Education Plans.

Accumulator II
Apple II
$175.00

A management system for special education that allows you to store and retrieve all information for each student. The program may be designed to fit each user's needs and allows up to twenty fields for each student. The company will allow a ten day preview of the program.

    Southern Microsystems For Education
    P.O. Box 1981
    Burlington, NC 27215
    (919) 226-7610

Braille Training Program
Apple II
$200.00

This program teaches and drills sighted persons in grade II Braille. Rules and contractions are displayed on the television screen. The user is presented with sample text to enter in Braille. The Apple keyboard acts like a Braillewriter and displays the entered Braille cells on the monitor. When the drill is ended, the computer compares the entered material with the correct version and displays any errors.

>Raised Dot Computing
>310 South 7th Street
>Lewisburg, PA 17837
>(717) 523-6739

Diascriptive Reading
Apple, Atari, PET, TRS-80
$295.00, set of seven disks

A diagnostic, prescriptive, tutorial reading program covering main idea, details, fact/opinion, vocabulary, sequence and inference at levels 3 through 8. The series contains six diagnostic tests and thirty-six developmental reading programs. The management system will keep track of the student's progress and will remediate or advance the student through each skill area without teacher intervention. Available on disk or cassette.

>Educational Activities, Inc.
>P.O. Box 392
>Freeport, NY 11520
>(800) 645-3739

The Evaluation System
Apple II Plus, Six Disks
$460.00

About one hundred programs on six diskettes that allow the rehabilitation specialist to assess rapidly the nonverbal, profoundly motor-handicapped individual in order to prescribe the optimal augmentative communication device. The system provides communication devices with graphic (Bliss symbol or Pictogram) and English vocabularies, with a variety of input methods (single, dual, triple, quad, or quint switches).

>I.O.R. Enterprises
>Route 6, Box 20
>Chapel Hill, NC 27514
>(919) 929-4825

Individual Educational Plans
Apple II, IIe, TRS-80, IBM
$1,500

Individual Educational Plans are generated after a student's evaluation. A one-page data sheet is completed with all of the information needed for an IEP. The company also produces supplementary programs and offers other related services.

>Learning Systems
>P.O. Box 15
>Marblehead, MA 01945
>(617) 639-0114

O'Brien Vocabulary Placement Test
Apple, Atari, PET, TRS-80
$24.95

A graduated vocabulary placement test that will find a student's independent reading level. Validated with over 7,000 students, it is culturally unbiased, discounts guessing and has a placement range of readiness through a 7th grade reading level. Also available on cassette for some computer models at $19.95.

>Educational Activities, Inc.
>P.O. Box 392
>Freeport, NY 11520
>(800) 645-3739

P.I.A.T. Error Analysis Report
Apple II
$395.00

Inputing results from the Peabody Individual Achievement Test along with individual information will produce a report containing:

1. student background information,
2. diagnostic statements indicating level of performance in the five skill areas measured on the P.I.A.T., and
3. a set of annual goals and short term objectives based on the pattern of errors on the P.I.A.T.

>Southern Microsystems For Education
>P.O. Box 1981
>Burlington, NC 27215
>(919) 226-7610

Project I.E.P.
Apple, Commodore
$1,495.00

A system to create, monitor and evaluate student I.E.P.s based on PL 94-142 regulations and School District Selected Special Education Program Objectives. Will store data on floppy disk or on hard disk systems. Project I.E.P. will print 15 different reports for teacher, parent, student and special education administrative review.

>Evans Newton Inc.
>7745 E. Redfield Road, Suite 100
>Scottsdale, AZ 85160
>(602) 998-2777

Special Education Administrative Software
Apple II, two disk drives
$375 to $650

Five programs may be combined to store data and reports for individual educational plans. I Data base student data and reports ($650), II conferences, IEP services, etc. ($375), III due process including referral assessment, reassessment and reports ($425), IV a report generator that produces individual and group reports ($485), V student incident system provides reports on student incidents ($425). Packages II through IV require I.

>Sysdata International, Inc.
>7671 Old Central Avenue NE
>Minneapolis, MN 55432
>(612) 780-1750

Special Educational Retrieval System
Apple II
$595.00, four disk set

The E.P.I. Retrieval System will allow you to locate quickly educational materials to meet the exact needs of your students. Approximately 5,000 of the most popular print materials from over one hundred publishers cover pre-K to adult education perceptual skills, motor skills, readiness, and beginning level of all basic skills. The system also allows you to include your own materials.

>Learning Well
>200 South Service Road
>Roslyn Heights, NY 11577
>(516) 621-1540

Test Of Syntactic Abilities
Apple II Plus, 48K
$75.00, two disk set

A nationally standardized test for prelingually deaf children from ten through eighteen years of age. Provides a profile of the student abilities in negation, conjunction, determiners, question formation, verb processes, pronominalization, relativization, complementation and nominalization. Available in two forms for pre- and post-testing. Forms are available individually at $39.95 each.

>Dormac, Inc.
>8034 Southwest Nimbus
>Beaverton, OR 97005
>(800) 547-8032

WISC-R Computer Report
Apple II
$495.00

Facilitates report writing or can be used as one component of the report. Enter the WISC-R Sub-Test scores, VIQ, PIQ, FSIQ as well as GE scores and standard scores of reading, spelling and arithmetic from an achievement test of your choice. The result will provide 70 to 90 percent of the final report.

>Southern Microsystems For Education
>P.O. Box 1981
>Burlington, NC 27215
>(919) 226-7610

Woodcock-Johnson Scoring Program
Apple II
$485.00

The program is designed for the first-time computer operator. Scoring of all twenty-seven subtests takes about ten minutes. Multiple copies of the report may be printed out. The report includes the cluster scoring completed for both grade and age, standard scores completed for both grade and age and functioning level completed for all cluster scores.

>Sysdata International, Inc.
>7671 Old Central Avenue, NE
>Minneapolis, MN 55432
>(612) 780-1750

Special Hardware Selections

G

Computers

Although most all microcomputers have been used in special education and by the handicapped, five stand out as being the most widely used. Nearly all of the standard educational software, specialized software, and hardware modifications run on at least one of these six microcomputer brands. They are the following.

Apple II Plus and Apple IIe
Apple Computer Company, Inc.
Education Division
20525 Mariani Ave.
Cupertino, CA 95014
(408) 996-1010

Atari 400, 800, 1200
Atari, Inc.
Home Computer Division
P.O. Box 61657
Sunnyvale, CA 94086
(800) 538-8547

IBM PC
IBM Corporation
Educational Marketing
P.O. Box 1328
Boca Raton, FL 33432
(404) 238-2208

PET, Vic, Commodore 64, CBM
Commodore Business Machines, Inc.
1200 Wilson Drive
West Chester, PA 19380
(215) 431-9100

Texas Instruments 99/4A, 99/2
Texas Instruments, Inc.
P.O. Box 10508
Lubbock, TX 79408
(806) 741-2000

TRS-80 Model III, Color Computer
Radio Shack
P.O. Box 2625
Fort Worth, TX 76113
(817) 390-3700

Special Input Devices

There are many alternative methods of controlling the microcomputer for those who would have difficulty using the keyboard. The simplest device may be a *keyguard*, which is a cover that fits over the keyboard. Holes are placed over each key position and serve as a guide for a finger, mouth stick or headpointer. The shift and control keys can be latched "on" for single finger control. Other persons may require special switches such as sip and puff, light beam, sound activated, radio controlled, tongue activated and others, as well as the interface from switch to computer. These devices are all available for the Apple from:

Prentke Romich Company
8769 Township Road 513
Shreve, OH 44676
(216) 567-2906

Keyboard emulators will produce individual characters and often preprogrammed words or phrases for input to the microcomputer without touching the keyboard. These devices usually present a panel of LEDs (Light Emitting Diodes) with each LED assigned to a specific character or command. The LEDs are scanned until a selection is made using any of the special switches mentioned above. The computer treats that input just as if it had come from the keyboard. One such product for the Apple II is:

TetraScan ($1,995.00)
Zygo Industries, Inc.
P.O. Box 1008
Portland, OR 97207
(503) 297-1724

A scanning technique for input can be directly imposed on standard software so that the special switches mentioned earlier, as well as Morse Code, can be used to control the program. This control is provided by a card that plugs into a slot in the Apple II.

Adaptive Firmware Card ($300)
Adaptive Peripherals
4535 Bagley Avenue North
Seattle, WA 98103
(206) 633-2601

Light pens can also be used for responding to choices presented on the computer screen. If the program has been written or modified to accept this type of input, the user only needs to touch the place on the screen displaying the proper choice with a penlike device connected to the computer. Light pens for the Apple II, PET and TRS-80 Models I & III are available from:

3G Company, Inc.
Route 3 Box 28A
Gaston, OR 97119
(503) 662-4492

Sound can also be used to control the microcomputer. It may be recognizable speech or any group of repeatable sounds. The speech input device is trained to recognize a specific sound and then output a character, command, or string of commands which the computer will accept as if it came from the keyboard. Two manufacturers of these devices are:

Shadow/VET ($995.00)
Scott Instruments
1111 Willow Springs Drive
Denton, TX 76201
(817) 387-9514

or

Voice Input Module ($825.00)
Voice Machine Communications, Inc.
10522 Covington Circle
Villa Park, CA 92667
(714) 639-6150

For the blind using Braille, two devices can produce Braille keyboarded material that will then run on the Apple II, provided proper translation software is used (see Raised Dot Computing). First is the VersaBraille, a paperless Brailler:

VersaBraille (approximately $6,000)
Telesensory Systems, Inc.
P.O. Box 10099
Palo Alto, CA 94304
(415) 493-2626

Second is a device most commonly understood as a stand-alone Braille embosser, the Perkins Brailler. It has been modified by the Kentucky Bureau For The Blind to drive or be driven by an Apple II. That modified version is being produced by:

Modified Perkins Brailler (approximately $2,500)
Maryland Computer Services, Inc.
2010 Rock Spring Road
Forest Hill, MD 20150
(301) 879-3366

Special Output Devices

In addition to the Braille devices listed above which function as input and output devices, it is possible to combine a pair of products meant for other uses to end up with a low-cost Apple II-driven Braille embosser. The output device itself is the Model D Braille typewriter, produced by IBM ($350.00). Driving the typewriter is ETF (Electric Typing Fingers), a solenoid and plunger device which accepts signals from the Apple and presses the keys on the typewriter. It is available from:

> *ETF* ($550.00)
> Personal Micro Computers, Inc.
> 475 Ellis Street
> Mountain View, CA 94043
> (415) 962-0220

Speech synthesizers provide fairly clear speech output from many programs without modification. Some software producers are also building in the necessary control software so that their program will produce speech with a specific brand of synthesizer. Two of the more popular brands are:

> *Echo* ($150.00 to $295.00)
> Street Electronics
> 1140 Mark Avenue
> Carpinteria, CA 93013
> (805) 684-4593
> or
> *Type-'N-Talk* ($375.00)
> Votrax Consumer Products Group
> 500 Stephenson Highway
> Troy, MI 48084
> (313) 588-2050

Miscellaneous Devices

For persons wishing to communicate over telephone lines with those using TTYs or TDDs using the Baudot code, there is one modem available for the Apple II that uses either ASCII or Baudot. It is:

> *Apple-Cat II* ($318.00 including deaf terminal software)
> Novation, Inc.
> 18664 Oxnard Street
> Tarzana, CA 91356
> (213) 996-5060

A speech trainer for the hearing impaired has been developed using a board that plugs into the Apple II and a special program. It produces a visual "graph" on the screen of words spoken into a microphone, first displaying the teacher's sample, then the student's attempts to match the sample. Contact:

Visible Speech For The Hearing Impaired ($675.00)
Software Research Corporation
University of Victoria
P.O. Box 1700
Victoria, B.C. V8W 2Y2
Canada

The Apple II can be used as a preprogrammed control device to operate up to 256 Levitron/BSR remote control devices, which may control appliances or any other electrically operated products. The control signals are sent over household powerlines. The PC-1 is available from:

PC-1 Powerline Controller ($340.00)
Bi-Comm Systems
10 Yorkton Industrial Court
St. Paul, MN 55117
(612) 481-0775

On-Line Services

H

On-line data base and communications services provide an incredibly powerful tool for the person interested in services and programs for the handicapped. The three services listed here contain many thousands of pages of data available at a reasonable charge and at electronic data transfer speed. Two of them also provide public and private communications, thereby allowing persons to exchange information. Any microcomputer equipped with a modem or acoustic coupler can access these systems.

BRS/After Dark
Bibliographic Retrieval Services
1200 Route 7
Latham, NY 12110
(518) 783-1161

Access thousands of pages of data and abstracts between 6 pm and midnight at a greatly reduced rate. Four of the data bases relevant to special education and the handicapped have a rate of $6.00 per hour, while one other is charged at $11.00 per hour. Users in 400 metro areas in the U.S. can access the system via a local telephone call. Powerful searching techniques reduce the amount of time needed on-line to locate data. In addition to the hourly rate, a registration fee of $50 is charged. A larger service with many more data bases and a much higher hourly rate is available during daytime business hours.

HEX (Handicapped Education Exchange)
Richard Barth
11523 Charlton Drive
Silver Spring, MD 20902
(301) 681-7372 (voice only)

A free bulletin board service dedicated to the education of and communication with the handicapped. Special education professionals and others interested in the field exchange information on the main bulletin board. Some articles and other data are available on the system as well. *HEX* accepts communications in ASCII or in Baudot, the code used by TTYs and TDDs. The telephone number used to gain access to the *HEX* bulletin board is (301) 593-7033.

SpecialNet
National Association of State Directors of Special Education
1201 16th Street, NW
Washington, DC 20036

A collection of seventeen bulletin boards allows persons to post and read messages on a wide variety of subjects related to special education. Some of the individual "boards" are primarily providers of information on selected topics, while others solicit input from the user. Electronic mail service is also part of the system. Many states have their own private "board" on this system also, thereby having private electronic communications between offices. The annual subscription fee is $200 per year. Usage fees range from $14 per hour to $4 per hour, depending on when the system is accessed.

Logo

Logo is available as a full computer programming language for the Apple II and IIe, Commodore 64, Atari 400, 800 and 1200XL with 16K cartridge, and the TI 99/4A home computers. There are a number of programs that offer turtle graphics for these and other brands of microcomputers but they do not have list processing capabilities or, in some cases, even print information on the screen. They may be less expensive but you are not getting a full Logo language.

Following is a list of the different manufacturers, the hardware requirements and the price information for full Logo language packages.

Apple Computer, Inc.
20525 Mariani Avenue
Cupertino, CA 95014
(800) 538-9696
(800) 662-9238 in CA

This product is the LCSI Logo. Designed for the Apple II, II plus with 16K language card and IIe, the system comes with two language disks. Print resources include the *Apple Logo: An Introduction to Programming Through Turtle Graphics* and *Apple Logo Reference Manual.* The cost of the package is $175.00.

Atari, Inc.
1265 Borregas Avenue
Sunnyvale, CA 94086
(800) 538-8543
(800) 672-1404 in CA

Once again, it's the LCSI Logo, but this time for the Atari 400, 800 and the 1200 XL, all with 16K cartridge. This package is scheduled for release in the fall of 1983 and should be priced under $100.00.

Commodore Computer
487 Devon Park Drive
Wayne, PA 19087
(215) 687-9750

Again, we have the M.I.T. Logo, this time for the Commodore 64 microcomputer. This version was created by Terrapin, Inc. for Commodore and the original enhancements unique to Terrapin versions have been included in this program. The language disk and manual are included.

Krell Software Corp.
1320 Stony Brook Road
Stony Brook, NY 11790
(516) 751-5139

This is another package based on the M.I.T. Logo. Hardware required is an Apple II or II plus with 48K and a 16K language card or a Franklin ACE 1000. Two language disks, utilities disk and the *Alice In Logoland Tutorial* is included. Print resources included are the *Logo for the Apple II* by Abelson and Klotz, an issue of *Logo Educational and Computing Journal*, and a wall chart. Price is $89.95.

Terrapin, Inc.
380 Green Street
Cambridge, MA 02139
(617) 492-8816

This is the M.I.T. Logo. It runs on an Apple II or IIe plus with 48K and a 16K language card, on the Franklin ACE 1000, and is also available for the AROS or Corvus Omninet networking systems. Software included in the package is the language disk along with a utilities disk that is extremely useful. One of the utilities allows single keystroke commands for use by very young or handicapped students. The *Terrapin Logo Tutorial* is filled with examples and is easy to use and includes a technical manual as well. Price is $149.95 for floppy disk and $300 for the hard disk version.

Texas Instruments
P.O. Box 53
Lubbock, TX 79408

This is the original microcomputer version of Logo. It runs on the TI 99/4A with memory expansion unit. The software included is the language cartridge along with TI Logo demonstration programs. This version of Logo has the famous Sprites. The *TI Logo Curriculum Guide* is included all for $129.95.

Logo Bibliography

The following bibliography is a list of periodicals, publications and books that will help you understand and use the LOGO language.

PERIODICALS CONTAINING ARTICLES ON LOGO

BYTE

"A Beginner's Guide to Logo" by Harold Abelson, August 82.

"Designing Computer-based Microworlds" by Robert Lawler, August 82.

"Introducing LOGO To Children" by Cynthia Solomon, August 82.

"LOGO—A Cultural Glossary" by E. Paul Goldenberg, August 82.

"LOGO: An Approach To Educating Disabled Children" by Weir, Russell, and Valente, September 82.

"LOGO For Personal Computers," by Harold Nelson, June 81.

"LOGO For The Apple II, The TI-99/4A, And The TRS-80 Color Computer" by Gregg Williams, August 82.

"LOGO In The Schools" by Dan Watt, August 82.

"The LOGO Journal, News And Views Of The Logo Community" a collection of articles, August 82.

"New Cultures From New Technologies" by Seymour Papert, September 81.

"Problem Solving With LOGO" by William Reinweb, November 82.

"Why LOGO?" by Brian Harvey, August 82.

Classroom Computer News

"The Beginner's Guide To LOGO" by Ricky Carter, April 83.

"Input/Output: Ideas From The Classroom" a collection of articles, April 83.

"Is There LOGO After Turtle Graphics?" by Tom Lough and Steve Tipps, April, 83.

"Learning With LOGO" by Dan Watt, April, 83.

Closing The Gap

A newspaper focusing on computer applications for the handicapped. Each issue has an article on LOGO by Griff and Robbie Wiggley.

Compute

Each issue contains a column called "Friends of the Turtle" by David Thornburg.

Computing Teacher

"Creating A LOGO Environment" by Tim Riordon, November 82.

"Learning LOGO And Liking It" by Rick Billstein, November 82.

"LOGO: A Computer Environment For Learning-Disabled Students" by Sylvia Weir and Dan Watt, volume 8, Number 5.

"LOGO and The Primary-Junior Pupil: One Student's First Encounter" by Rena Uptis, November 82.

"LOGO's List Handling Abilities" December 82.

"Microworlds" by Glenn Bull, November 82.

"The Million Dollar Smile" by Jim Muller, February 83.

"Papert At The Faire" by Merrianne Coon, November 82.

"Teaching Turtles" by Kathleen Martin and Andrew Berner, November 82.

"TI LOGO And First Graders—A Winning Combination" by Nellie Bandelier, November 82.

"Turtle Graphics On And Off The Computer" by Kathleen Martin, Donna Bearden and James Muller, November 82.

"Turtle Talk" by Rena Uptis, November 82.

"Watercross: A LOGO Exploration" by Tom Lough, November 82.

"What Can The Computer And The Young People's LOGO Association Do For Handicapped Children?" by Jim Muller, November 82.

Beginning with the January 83 issue, a feature called *The LOGO Center* appears monthly. It is written by Kathleen Martin and Tim Riordon.

Book Reviews: *Apple LOGO/LOGO For The Apple II*, by Harold Abelson, reviewed by Jim McCauley, and *Turtle Geometry* by Abelson and diSessa, reviewed by Rick Billstein, November 82.

Creative Computing

"A Comparison of The Problem Solving Styles of Two Students Learning LOGO" by Dan Watt, December 79.

"Computers And Computer Cultures" by Seymour Papert, March 81.

"The Friendly Languages" by Jim Muller, October 81.

"Seymour Papert And The LOGO Universe" by Richard Eyster, December 81.

"What Is LOGO?" by Molly Watt, October 82.

Each issue contains a column on Logo by Robert Lawler.

Educational Computer

"Widening Learning Horizons With TI LOGO" by Grace Mason, January-February 82.

Electronic Learning

A comparison of each version of LOGO, March 83.

Instructor

"Computers Are Objects To Think With" an interview with Seymour Papert, March 81.

"LOGO Fever: The Computer Language Every School Is Catching" January 83.

Microcomputing (formerly Kilobaud Microcomputing)

"Learning With LOGO At The Lamplighter School" by six Lamplighter Teachers, September 81.

"LOGO: Not Just For Kids" by Harold Nelson, March 82.

"LOGO And The Exceptional Child" by Sylvia Wier, September 81.

"LOGO And The Great Debate" by Richard Carter, September 81.

"Through A New Looking Glass" by Henry Olds, September 81.

"Whither Goes The Turtle?" by J. Rousseau and S. Smith, September 81.

Personal Computing

"Progressive Learning By Computer" by Steven Berry, December 81.

Popular Computing (formerly Oncomputing)

"Learning With LOGO" by Harold Nelson, Summer 81.

"Seymour Papert: Spearheading The Computer Revolution" by Nelson and Friedman, Summer 81.

"Should Children Be Computer Programmers?" by Dan Watt, September 82.

Popular Mechanics
"LOGO and Personal Computers" September 82.

Softalk
"LOGO, The Voice Of The Turtle" by Jim Muller, July 82.
> Jim Muller has a regular column on Logo in *Softalk*.

Softside
"Apple LOGO/LOGO For The Apple II" by Harold Abelson, reviewed by Steve Birchall, volume 6, Number 3.

"LOGO: The Programmer-Friendly Language" by Steve Birchall, volume 6, Number 3

99'er Magazine
"Extending LOGO: Applications For Very Young Children" by Henry Gorman, volume 1, Number 4.

"The Lamplighter LOGO Project" by Henry Gorman, May-June, 81.

"LOGO: A Computer Language As A Learning Environment" by Dan Watt, May-June 81.

"LOGO's Powerful Surprises" by Roger Kirchner, volume 1, Number 4.

Each month's issue contain one or more articles on TI Logo by Henry Gorman and Roger Kirchner.

BOOKS/INSTRUCTIONAL GUIDES ON LOGO

Apple LOGO/LOGO For The Apple II, by Harold Abelson, BYTE/McGraw-Hill, 1982.

Apple Logo Primer and *CyberLogo Primer* by Garry Bitter and Nancy Watson, Reston Publishing Company, Reston, VA.

CyberLogo Turtle: A First Step In Computer Literacy, by Cybertronics, International, Reston Publishing Company, Reston, VA.

Learning With LOGO, by Dan Watt, BYTE/McGraw-Hill, 1983.

LOGO: A Problem Solving Approach, by Joan Davis and Joan Schenker, Turtle Enterprise North, 11515 Kathy Drive, Spokane, WA.

LOGO: An Introduction For Teachers, by Dr. J. Dale Burnett, Faculty of Education, Queen's University, Kingston, Ontario, K7L 3N6, Canada.

Mindstorms: Children, Computers and Powerful Ideas, by Seymour Papert, Basic Books, 1980.

One, Two, Three, My Computer And Me: A LOGO Funbook for Kids, by Donna Beardon/Young People's LOGO Association, Reston Publishing Company, Reston, VA.

Special Technology For Special Children, by E. Paul Goldenberg, University Park Press, 1979.

Turtle Geometry: The Computer As A Medium For Exploring Mathematics, by Harold Abelson and Andrea diSessa, MIT Press, 1981.

The Turtle's Sourcebook, by Jim Muller, Donna Bearden, Kathleen Martin, Young People's LOGO Association, 1208 Hillsdale Drive, Richardson, TX.

ORGANIZATION NEWSLETTERS AND OTHER PUBLICATIONS

Turtle New and The Logo Newsletter
Monthly publication of the Young People's Logo Association, 1208 Hillsdale Drive, Richardson, TX 75081.

Polyspiral
Newsletter of the Boston Computer Society's Logo User Group.

National Logo Exchange
Monthly publication aimed at those teaching Logo, P.O. Box 5341, Charlottesville, VA 22905.

Logo And Educational Computing Journal
Krell Software Corporation, 1320 Stony Brook Road, Stony Brook, NY 11790.

TI Source And Logo News
Newspaper on TI products and TI Logo, Microcomputers Corporation, 34 Maple Avenue, Armonk, NY 10504.

Massachusetts Institute of Technology
The Division for Study and Research in Education-Logo Group has over sixty Memos on Logo as it was developed through the 1970s. Of particular interest is The Final Report of the Brookline Logo Project, Parts II and III, by Dan Watt, Seymour Papert, Andrea diSessa, and Sylvia Weir, September 79, (Memos 53 and 54). For a free bibliography of all the Memos write: Logo Group: D.S.R.E., MIT, 10C-109, 77 Massachusetts Avenue, Cambridge, MA 02139.

FOLLK, (Friends of LISP, Logo and Kids)
San Francisco State University, 436 Arballo Drive, San Francisco, CA 94132.

Friends Of The Turtle
c/o David Thornburg, P.O. Box 1317, Los Altos, CA 94022.

Logophile
An occasional newsletter edited by Dr. William Higginson, Faculty of Education, Queen's University, Kingston, Ontario, K7L 3N6, Canada.

Print Resource

One of the best ways to stay abreast of software and hardware developments are the magazines, newspapers and newsletters published in the education and computer fields. Many of these periodicals review software and hardware on a regular basis.

BYTE

A monthly magazine (about 625 pages per month) covering general computer applications. Subscription rate is $19.00 per year. A McGraw-Hill Publication, 70 Main St., Peterborough, NH 03458.

Closing The Gap

A newspaper dealing with microcomputers in special education and for the handicapped. Software and hardware reviews are regular features as well as new product information, articles on applications, etc. It is published six times per year with a subscription fee of $15.00. Published by Budd and Dolores Hagen, P.O. Box 68, Henderson, MN 56044.

Compute

A monthly, dealing with general microcomputer applications for the Atari, Pet and Apple microcomputers. Subscription rate is $20.00 per year. P.O. Box 5406, Greensboro, NC 27403.

Computer Classroom News

Emphasis is on application of microcomputers in the classroom. Subscription rate is $16.00 per year. Published by Intentional Educations, Inc., 51 Spring Street, Watertown, MA 02172.

Computerworld

A weekly newspaper convering general computer subjects, published by Computerworld, Inc., 797 Washington Street, Newton, MA 02160.

Computing Teacher, The

This publication is produced nine times a year by the Oregon Council for Computer Education. The content is designed by and for educators interested in microcomputer use in the classroom. Subscription rate is $14.50 per year with a $2.25 cover price. Department of Computer and Information Science, University of Oregon, Eugene, OR 97403.

Creative Computing

Monthly magazine covering general uses of microcomputer technology. Software and hardware evaluations appear regularly. Subscription rate is $20.00 per year. P.O. Box 789-M, Morristown, NJ 07960.

Educational Computer

Educational use of microcomputers in the classroom as well as administrative applications. Six issues per year with a $15.00 subscription fee. P.O. Box 535, Cupertino, CA 95015.

80 Micro

A TRS-80 specific general information magazine. One year subscription is $24.97. P.O. Box 981, Farmingdale, NY 11737.

Electronic Education

Published nine times each year, September through March. Features educational uses of the microcomputer. Subscriptions are $18.00 per year. Electronic Communications, Inc., Suite 220, 1311 Executive Center Drive, Tallahassee, FL 32301.

Electronic Learning

A Scholastic, Inc. publication dealing with educational uses of technology. Five issues per year for $17.00 subscription fee. 902 Sylvan Avenue, Englewood Cliffs, NJ 07632.

InCider
Apple specific publication issued twelve times per year for $25.00 per year. General applications for the Apple user. 80 Pine St., Peterborough, NH 03458.

InfoWorld
A newsweekly for general microcomputer uses. Subscriptions are available for $25.00 per year. Published by Popular Computing, Inc., 375 Cochituate Road, Box 880, Framingham, MA 01701.

Journal of Computer-Based Instruction
A quarterly publication of the Association for Development of Computer-based Instructional Systems. The *Journal* prints articles on research and theory of CAI and CMI. Subscription rate is $12.00 for nonmembers. Western Washington University, Bellingham, WA 98225.

The Mathematics Teacher and The Arithmetic Teacher
Published by the National Council of Teachers of Mathematics. Eight issues per year. 1906 Association Drive, Reston, VA 22091.

Microcomputers in Education QUEUE
A Newsletter published twelve times per year. Subscription is $15.00. 5 Chapel Hill Drive, Fairfield, CT 06432.

Nibble
Apple specific publication that gives hardware and software tips for general uses of Apple computers. Published eight times a year for $17.50. P.O. Box 325, Lincoln, MA 01773.

PC
An IBM specific magazine for general microcomputer uses. Subscription is $26.97 per year. 39 E. Hanover Ave., Morrisplaines NJ 07950.

Personal Computing
General microcomputer magazine for TRS-80, Pet and Apple users. 12 issues with a subscription fee of $14.00. 1050 Commonwealth Avenue, Boston, MA 02215.

Popular Computing
General microcomputer user magazine published 8 times a year. (Formerly On Computing). Published by McGraw-Hill, 70 Main Street, Peterborough, NH 03458.

Softalk

Apple specific publication with a lot of good general information, articles, etc. Free to Apple owners for one year. Send your serial number to Softalk, 11021 Magnolia Blvd., North Hollywood, CA 91601.

Index

A

ASCII, 43, 48, 60
ASL (American Sign Language) 41
Access, 15, 17
Acoustic coupler, 8
Adaptive Firmware Card, 59
American Telephone & Telegraph, 9, 44
Art, 86
Association for Retarded Citizens, 55
Authoring systems, 6, 7, 23

B

BASIC, 2, 26, 28
BRS, 81
Babies, 89
Baudot, 43, 48
Behrmann, Mike, 89
Bernstein, Saul, 86
Blind, 13, 49, 77
Bliss symbols, 58, 61

Braille, 49, 77
Braille-Edit, 49, 50
Bulletin board, 47

C

CAI (Computer Assisted Instruction) 3, 14
Cavalier, Dr. Al, 56
CCD (Cassette Control Device) 37
Cerebral palsy, 11, 61
Closing the Gap, 61, 62, 68, 98
Communication, 8, 19, 41, 61, 72
Compatability, 21
Computer literacy, 3
Computer revolution, 74, 96
Courseware, 6, 7

D

Deaf, 9, 29, 41, 48, 66
Drill and practice, 34, 36

E

E-Mail (electronic mail) 78
E-Z Pilot, 26, 51
Echo II, 37
Environmental control, 10, 11, 89

F

Family Computer Center, 67
Future, 12, 89

G

Game controller, 16, 59
Games, 15, 18, 59
George Mason University, 89

H

HERO-I, 93
HEX (Handicapped Educational Exchange) 82
Handicapped Typewriter, 16
Hearing impaired, 41, 45
Holladay, David, 50
Home, 95

I

IQ, 54, 57
Information age, 74, 78, 94
Interactive video, 93, 94

J

Jenkins, Sam, 54, 56
Johns Hopkins, 31, 43

K

Keyboard emulators, 17, 59
Keyboard, 15, 54, 60
Keyguards, 15

L

Lahm, Liz, 89
Language handicapped, 39
Language with a purpose, 79
Learning disabled, 6, 13, 18, 33, 38
Letter identification, 54
Loan program, 44
Logo, 7, 8, 27, 28, 57, 65

M

MCE, Inc., 57
MECC, 76, 94
Major Authoring Systems, 26
Mentally retarded, 53
Micro Quest, 24, 25

Mini-Authoring System, 24
Modem, 8
Morse code, 60
Motivation, 6, 15, 18, 34
Music, 86

N

Northern Bell, 44

O

On-line, 4, 73, 77, 81

P

PILOT, 26
PLATO, 76
Paint, 88
Parents, 95
Pencil & Paper Blockade, 38, 40, 78
Perkins Brailler, modified, 51
Physically handicapped, 58, 77, 89
Picture-Com., 58
Printers, 39, 40
Problem solving, 7, 27, 28, 67, 69
Program R.E.A.C.T., 84
Programming, 2, 6, 28, 71

R

Raised Dot Computing, 49, 52
Robotics, 93

S

SPIN/SPIF, 81
Scan routine, 58, 59, 62
School without walls, 95
Scott Instruments, 63
Self expression, 7, 27, 65, 69
Seyfried, David, 62
Shadow/VET, 63

Software previewing, 23
Software, 3, 5, 21, 36
Spasticity, 15
Special Net, 81
Special Technology for Special Children, 27, 40, 58
Speech impaired, 44
Speech synthesis, 37, 49, 52, 54, 56, 62
Sports, 84
Switches, 11, 16, 58, 62, 72, 90

T

TDD-TTY, 9, 43, 46, 48
TMR, 53
Telecommunication, 9, 29, 43, 45, 79
Timeshare, 75
Turtle Graphics, 66
Typing skills, 5, 15, 40, 83
Typing tutor, 5, 15, 40, 46, 83

U

University of Wisconsin/Stout, 54, 56
User control, 36

V

VersaBraille, 49
Visually impaired, 49
Vocalization training, 43
Voice entry, 17, 63
Voice output, See speech synthesis 102
Votrax Type 'N Talk, 90

W

Weitbrecht, Bob, 43
Word processing, 38
Written language, 38, 45, 48, 62, 78

Y

Young Peoples' Logo Association, 67, 69